THE ROOTS OF THE BLUES

D0619761

An African Search

Alhaji Sait Camara

THE ROOTS
OF THE BLUES

AN AFRICAN SEARCH

SAMUEL CHARTERS

A DA CAPO PAPERBACK

Library of Congress Cataloging in Publication Data

Charters, Samuel Barclay.
  The roots of the blues: an African search / Samuel Charters.
     p.   cm. — (Da Capo paperback)
  Reprint. Originally published: Boston: M. Boyars, 1981.
  ISBN 0-306-80445-X
  1. Blues (Music) — History and criticism. 2. Music — Africa, West —
History and criticism. I. Title.
  [ML3521.C5 1991]   91-20452
  781.643'09 — dc20   CIP

This Da Capo Press paperback edition of *The Roots of the Blues*
is an unabridged republication of the edition published in Salem,
New Hampshire in 1981. It is reprinted by arrangement with
Marion Boyars, Inc.

Published by Da Capo Press, Inc.
A Subsidiary of Plenum Publishing Corporation
233 Spring Street, New York, N.Y. 10013

For Betty and Martin Colyer

A Note

All of the music described in this book can be heard on albums released from field recordings done on my trips to West Africa. A broad survey called 'African Journey – Volumes 1 and 2' has been released by Sonet Records in London and by Vanguard Records in New York. A collection of griot songs by Jali Nyama Suso, called 'Songs of The Gambia', has also been released by Sonet Records. The longer griot narratives, including 'Toolongjong' by Alhaji Fabala Kanuteh, are available on a double album set titled 'The Griots' released by Folkways Records in New York. Folkways has also issued an album of flute music played by musicians of the Serrehule and Fula tribes. The title is 'African Flutes'.

I would like to express my sincere thanks to Dag Haeggqvist, Gunnar Bergstrom and Sven Lindholm, directors of Sonet Grammoton AB, Stockholm, Sweden, who have given sympathetic support to many of my research and recording projects over the last ten years.

Samuel Charters

West Africa

CONTENTS

1   To The Gambia   1

2   A Mandingo Jali   10

3   'I Can Tell You The History of Everything'   23

4   A River Place   34

5   Toolongjong   47

6   Some Young Griots   53

7   Drums In The Streets   66

8   A Meeting With Slavery   78

9   'The Province of Freedom'   96

10   A Creole Village   110

11   The African Blues Roots   119

12   A Sense of Something Older   127

13   The Bamako-Dakar International Express   137

14   A Bridge Over The Niger   146

With photographs by the author

... When the Europeans came,
when they brought their ship from Portugal,
the ship used to start its journey from Banjul,
then it went to Sanumunko Jammeh, and Mansa Demba Sanko,
and Samkala Marong, and Wali Mandeba, and Jata Sela.
Anyone who had slaves they collected them all together
and took them to the places called Aladabara and Jufure
to sell them to the Portuguese.
Then the Portuguese put them in their ship
and left there and went to Jang Jang Bure.
When they arrived there they went
right to the slave house to collect slaves there
and take them to the Hollanders.
Then the Hollanders collected them and sent them to America.
It is because of this
that slaves are plenty in America.

They call them American Negroes.

From *The Song of Alhaji Fabala Kanuteh*

1

To The Gambia

I have some difficulty in describing why I travelled to West Africa and what I was doing there, since the journey that became so complicated and took me to so many unexpected places seemed — in the beginning — to be so simple and so clearly defined. I went to Africa to find the roots of the blues. It had always been obvious that the blues sprang from a complex cultural background, with much of it developing from the music of the long period of African slavery in the United States, and with some of its harmonic forms and instrumental styles derived out of a broad European context. It had always been just as obvious that there were certain elements in the blues — in the singing style and in the rhythmic structures — that weren't traceable to anything in the countryside of the American South. These things, it seemed to me, might have come from a distantly remembered African background, even if there had been such a lengthy period between the break in contact with Africa and the emergence of the blues in the 1890s. It was these aspects of the earliest blue styles that I was searching for in West Africa.

In the beginning I planned simply to record the West African tribal singers known as griots, since it was these musicians who seemed to come the closest to what we know as a blues singer. They are from tribes that had many people taken to the southern states as slaves, and they usually sing alone, accompanying themselves for the most part on plucked string instruments. Since most African music is performed by village groups, and is often dominated by drumming, this in itself is enough to set the griots apart. Each West African tribe has its own griot singers, and they perform in styles shaped by their own distinct tribal cultures, but I thought that perhaps in their music I could find some of the elements that had become part of the blues. At the same time I hoped to collect from the singers narrative accounts of the first encounters between the Africans and the Europeans, told from the African viewpoint. I felt that this could give me a clearer picture of one of the factors that had shaped the early black experience in the United States.

Before leaving for Africa I'd spent months taking notes on the tribal groups and areas that had been important as the source of slaves for the American South, and I'd also worked with as much material on the griots as I could find. As I traveled I had a definite idea of where I wanted to go, but at the same time I hadn't planned the trip in any way. There are two ways to travel: one with a clear and detailed itinerary and the other with simply the willingness to follow suggestions and ideas. I've always felt that to plan a trip too carefully is to make sure you won't find out anything you don't already know.

I didn't know, however, how much the simple trip I had begun would change direction once I'd come to Africa, almost as if it took on a life and a will of its own. I began to feel like someone who'd bought a set of boxes that fit inside each other in a wooden nest. When I opened one there was another, and inside that was still another. I found so many boxes inside each other that the simple project I had begun with became a series of new perceptions, each of which was contained within the perception – the box – that I'd just opened. Sometimes, as I sat on sagging beds engulfed in dusty mosquito nets the space around me seemed to be filled with the myriad boxes of different sizes that my notebooks and tapes had come to symbolize.

When I opened the box that was the music I'd come to record I found that the box inside that was slavery itself. There was no way that I could work with the music without taking into consideration how it had come to the United States. I also realized that this was one of the reasons I had come to Africa. I wanted to find out what the attitude toward slavery was for the Africans themselves. This meant that the trip became more complicated since I wasn't looking for something specific, like a style of music. I wasn't even searching for something as definite as the kind of interrelationships that an anthropologist looks for. I was trying to find traces of an *experience*, and not only that, I was looking for traces of an experience that had occurred hundreds of years before. Would what I found have any reality for me so many years afterward?

I understand now that this complex set of questions had already been there in my mind when I put the microphones and the tape recorder into my shoulder bag. I had always tried to have some conception of the slavery that had brought the West Africans to the United States, even if I hadn't seen, symbolically, that when I opened the box decorated with pictures of musicians and instruments inside it would be the next box, illustrated with old engravings of the slave ships and the slave caravans. I could have stopped at that point, and that is the point where most work has stopped. But, as I said, I hadn't planned my journey. As I travelled I let myself be led by other people's suggestions and my own moods.

Whatever there is to be said for the old way of coming to West Africa by sea – the easy tempo of the slow boat stopping at the coastal ports, the cool ocean winds, the chance to talk and read – the airplane has not only the advantage of being so much faster. If you're coming to Africa for the first time the plane journey helps to establish the dimensions of the land in your mind. Its size begins to have a meaning, the textures of the landscape take on a distinctiveness and a changing variety. As the plane leaving Europe behind comes over the Spanish peninsula and slips across the gray green rivulet of the Straits of Gibraltar you see first the sweeping crescent of the coastline of North Africa and its white lip of foam that's clearly visible from the plane's altitude. Morocco, in the winter months, is composed of dark tones of brown and gray-blue, with straggling clusters of village houses and to the east the snow crested outline of the Atlas mountains. It seems bare and thin, the brownness of the landscape startling after Europe's lush green hues. Then the sparseness of the landscape sliding slowly away below the plane trickles out until there isn't even sparseness, there is only the emptiness of the desert.

As you look down at the desert, however, it isn't entirely empty, and it's these small tokens of life that give the desert its intensity. Stretching like thin lines of thread you can see winding trails crossing a yellow brown waste that looks as uninhabitable as the surface of a distant planet. The lines of old caravan trails meander up and down the stony plateaus, through eroded dead stream beds, without any place – even from the plane's high perch – that seems to offer food or water. There, slipping out of the haze, you can see the scattered shapes of buildings at an oasis – but then the trail begins its tireless meandering again out into the pitted, dessicated surface, and again you can't see any place that it might be leading to. Even knowing that the Sahara once was greener and that the old caravan trails were well marked and traveled you still have the feeling that hundreds of men and animals must have died on that dead land trying to find their way to the next water, the next grass.

Despite the plane's height, the heat of the desert seems to spread itself through the cabin as the hours drift slowly past and the desert trails lifeless and unending below you. Despite the plane's air conditioning people up and down the aisle languidly fan themselves. The map of West Africa that you spread out on your lap suggests that the Senegal River should mark some kind of boundary, that there should be some signs of life along it, and before you reach it there are the first wavering circles of the tribal compounds, looking like worn dirt rings that someone has carelessly drawn on the pale brown earth. The river itself is a sombre green form lying inert in the haze. I had expected to see villages and cultivated fields lining its banks, but the water is too saline to be used for irrigation and it's allowed to slip away toward the ocean. South of the river I began to see the groups of Wollof villages, and finally the sharp lines that marked the European roads and the stiff patterns of the small inland cities.

The plane drifts back toward the coast as it crosses Senegal, and you become conscious of the choking tangle of vegetation that fills the mouths of the streams that reach the ocean, even though the country inland is dusty and brown. There had been a semblance of green close to the hut areas, but it was the end of the dry season and the brown tone of withered grass and strips of bushes lay over the earth beneath me. The plane was now south of the cultivated area of Senegal, and the landscape was irregularly marked with the ring-shaped compounds. The plane began to drop toward the flat plain along the coast and then circled over the tangle of growth that lines the banks of the Gambia River, winding across the countryside below. The shapes of trees became visible as we dropped lower, then the outlines of cultivated fields and small buildings. The land south of the Gambia River is flat and sandy, and the vegetation is sparse, even in the rainy season, but it was less overgrown now and the small cattle that had become visible seemed to be grazing over a large, poorly tended park.

The narrow landing runway that had been slashed out of the dusty countryside was covered with a rusted metal web of plating and the plane landed with a crash that sounded as if something had shattered inside the fuselage. As it slowed down, the plane lurched over the uneven surface of the plating as though a landing gear had been bent when we hit. But the plane made its unsteady way to a small parking area at the edge of the runway and a gang of men and boys began pushing a battered landing ramp out towards us. The customs officials and immigration service officers, who had set up tables under the trees to process the arrival, moved some of the crowd of loiterers out of the way so that we could officially be welcomed to The Gambia.

One thing you certainly become conscious of as you fly over Africa is its size. Africa is vast. It's so large that the United States could be dropped into the desert I had flown over and there would be still a sandy rim left around the edge. Even knowing the areas where I wanted to work — and even more definitely the tribal groups I wanted to be with — I still had the problem of finding a place where I could come closest to the singers and their culture. It was finally The Gambia that seemed to be the most promising. Perhaps — again a paradox — because in the empty spaces of the West African plain The Gambia is so small. Until the Europeans established themselves in a kind of uneasy permanence on the West African coast in the 19th Century, the coastal areas had been almost deserted. Because of this, the view we have of those countries today is hopelessly distorted. The cities that are there now have nothing to do with the older African cultures, which were hundreds, sometimes thousands, of miles inland. They don't even represent any kind of real African culture today. They were put there simply because there was some kind of harbor where boats could land. Usually there is no good farming land close to them, often the amount of land in the vicinity is inadequate for growth, and often they were placed in areas considered too disease-ridden to be habitable. Much of the dismal oppressiveness of the cities of West Africa is easier to understand if this is remembered.

At its mouth the Gambia River looks as though it opens into the center of Africa. The first European travelers to reach it, however, found quickly that it doesn't go very far inland, and that it doesn't have access to any sizeable population area; so Banjul, the capital city of The Gambia, has never grown as Dakar or Abidjan or Lagos have grown. Banjul is supposed to have a population of about thirty-five thousand people, but it seems even smaller. It is so badly situated that it has almost no place to expand, and sprawling villages not far from the airport have begun to overtake it in size. The entire country, however, has only about five hundred thousand people; so there isn't the heavy pressure on the city that the larger coastal cities like Accra or Lagos have to cope with.

But this smallness, for me, was an advantage. It was much easier for me to make my way around Banjul than it would have been in one of the larger cities where there were hundreds of thousands of people living in desperate squalor. At the same time here were the cultural groups I needed to work with. The city and the villages close to it had filled with Mandingo, Wollof, and Fula peoples, the groups whose musicians I wanted to document, the tribes that had been part of the wave of slaves taken to the United States. Also The Gambia had been an English colony and it wasn't as easy for me to communicate with people in the former French colonies since my own French is limited. Out in the countryside I found this made little difference since the village people usually spoke their own tribal language. If they had a second language it was usually that of one of the neighboring tribes. The European languages are generally limited to people in the towns, and even there the knowledge is often rudimentary. As Senegal, a former French colony, and The Gambia try endlessly to find some way of cooperating with each other, the two governments send official groups to meet their opposite numbers in the other government and a Gambian official described a meeting to me where the Senegalese delegation, who had been sent on cultural matters, presented their ideas in French. When they'd finished one of the Gambians asked, 'Why didn't you speak Wollof, so we could understand you?'

I had, then, a place to begin working: this river course in southern Senegal, which for long and complex reasons had become English instead of French. Of all the anomalies that colonialism has left on the African landscape there is none that's stranger than The Gambia. It is, literally, only a water course. The country is 295 miles long and between fifteen and thirty miles wide. Since the Gambia River is so sluggish and mud choked, there isn't even the semblance of a river valley. There is just the brown presence of the river, with its course in some places marked by low hills beyond its mud banks. It was an English colony for many years, and it still is uneasily English in many of its outlooks, despite the presence of Senegal which practically surrounds it. The first travelers from Europe to see the river were Portuguese in 1445, but their presence was brief and casual. Except for a new shape for building huts which the Mandingo learned from the Portuguese traders who lived along the river, the African cultures were unchanged by contact with the Portuguese.

It's almost meaningless to follow Europe's dynastic wars, but each of them seemed to leave some mark on the surface of the earth thousands of miles away. Already Europe's development of newer technologies was beginning to cast its lengthening shadow over the world's less developed societies. An internal struggle within Portugal over the succession to the throne led to the usurpation of power by the king of Spain, and an illegitimate son of a Portuguese royal prince who had been driven to England began selling trading concessions along the river to English merchants. What did a trading concession, in itself, mean? Not much. Only the right to engage in trade in a specified area, something like an arrangement to be a manufacturer's representative. But for the English it did mean a way around the Papal demarcation of 1493, which had ceded the area to Portugal. The first English ships sailed up the river in 1587 and came back to England with a profitable cargo of hides and ivory. It wasn't until later that the trade in slaves began.

Even with the English, Dutch and French involved in the trade along the river the activity was sporadic and only occasionally profitable. The banks of the Gambia, behind their tangle of vegetation were thinly settled. The river is so sluggish that it is still tidal for more than a hundred miles of its course, which means that like the Senegal River the water is too saline to be used for cultivation. At the mouth of the river, which is only a series of desolate, shifting sandbars at the edge of the mangrove swamp, there was almost no population at all until the beginning of the nineteenth century. The English trading station was on a small island twenty miles upstream. It was only after the decision was made to end the slave trade that the English, in 1806, built a settlement along the river's banks close to where it flows into the sea.

It was to this settlement – which had eventually become the city of Banjul – that I first came in February, 1974. By the time papers and passports had been examined by the Customs officials and the baggage had been unloaded and put on the ground close to the buses waiting to take us into Banjul, it was already late afternoon. Most of us had found a place to sit on the ground in the shade of the trees which had been planted outside the airport's waiting room, and we spent the time trying to wave away the hordes of small boys and vendors who offered us badly made carvings or fans or belts or strings of beads. As we went on refusing they became more and more persistent and exasperating until one of the policemen helping the Customs men came and chased them away. After a few moments they slowly crept back and the whole thing started all over again. Most of the other people around me were Swedish and Danish tourists who had come to lie on the beaches at the handful of hotels which had been built for them on the coast south of the river. I was continually surprised when small African boys came up and asked me, in recognizable Swedish, whether I was Swedish or Danish. There were some tables and chairs in the waiting room, but they were taken up with more or less suntanned Swedish secretaries clinging to the young Gambians who had become their companions for the week. Often the girls were crying, while the young men fingered their new jewelry and looked sleepily over the girls' shoulders at the new arrivals.

Since I was going into the town itself, my bus was the last to leave, and we set off across the countryside just as the sun was setting. I could see that we were passing through flat, poor land, with the occasional stucco house alternating with native huts made of sticks and mud. The horizon was lined with the forlorn fringe of palm trees, and the ditches along the much-repaired roadway were choked with weeds and bushes. The country had a shabby, desolate look that I was to become used to before I had done much more travelling. This was the physical setting – the Africa I had come to see.

By the time we reached the bridge that led into Banjul it was too dark to see more than the shadows of the mangrove swamp that had choked off the city's growth, but the scent of leaves and water rose from it, mingling with a smell of peanuts – The Gambia's main agricultural product – that seemed to hover over everything. Since I was staying alone in a simple hotel the bus stopped only long enough for me to get my bags out of the luggage compartment. I was left at the back of a large, dark building that I gathered from a dim sign on the wall was the hotel. I picked up my bags, slung them over my shoulders and looked around, impatient for the morning to come so I could begin.

2

A Mandingo Jali

For the first week I was so unused to the West African sun that I found
it almost impossible to go out in the middle of the day. Certainly I
wasn't the first traveler to The Gambia to be overwhelmed by it. One
of the early English adventurers to drop anchor in the river, Robert
Holmes, set out in 1661 with a small ship's party to meet the King of
Kombo, and they had to walk ten miles through the midday sun to
reach the king's village. It was the heat that Holmes talked about most
when he later wrote about the journey.

> It was a very hott day — no breath of wind stirring. The king
> accomodated me with the only horse that there was to be hadd, but
> being young and strong, and Captain Stokes old, fatt, and burley, I let
> him ride and I walked, which was one of the hardest tasks I ever
> undertook, the sun shineing so very hott, and all our way upon dry
> sand. It was soe very hott that our chirurgeons mate, whom I took
> along with me for fear of any accident ... fell down dead upon the
> way, and soe did a greyhound I had with me. Nay, one Mr Fowler,
> walking along with me, carrying a gun upon his shoulder, the excessive
> heat of the sun fired it from his shoulder. I was 3 or 4 daies so dazed in
> my head I thought I should never have recovered.*

As impatient as I was to begin working with the griots I couldn't face
the sun between ten in the morning and three in the afternoon. It was
only early in the morning or late in the afternoon that I could talk with
people in the government offices who knew where I might find the
singers. A few days after I arrived in Banjul, one of the men working
for the Gambian national radio service, a young Fula named Musa
Camara, offered to take me to meet one of the best-known Mandingo
griots or jalis, as they're called in their own language. The jali lived in
a village called Bakau, about twelve miles south of Banjul on the
Atlantic coast. Musa felt it would be best to go in the middle of the
day; since he was sure the jali would be in the village then. The only
way to the jali's compound, however, was a foot path across the fields

* Lady Sothorn, The Gambia, The Story of the Groundnut Colony (London, George
Allen & Unwin, 1926), p. 64.

behind the village and I found myself stumbling after Musa's disappearing figure through a haze of numbing heat. The earth around me had been burnt over as part of the cycle of crop cultivation, but the sun's glare was so intense that it seemed it must have been the sun itself that had left the landscape blackened with charred tree limbs and the stubble of brown, withered grass. The air was filled with an acrid scent of burning that mingled with the smells of the path's fiery dust and the village's sewage.

Bakau itself was a loose collection of huts and trees that sprawled over the roads that had once marked its edge. It was so much the color of the earth, its shapes so low and indistinct, that it seemed to be growing out of the bushes around it. As I walked into the shadows of the village along the hardened earth of the path, the outline of the buildings faded into sagging rows of rusting corrugated iron that lined the twisting path. The buildings were grouped together in compounds which were shielded behind fences as tall as my head. All I could see was the uneven line of the path, the dust covered leaves of the bushes and trees that leaned over the fences of the compounds, the worn wooden sticks of the fence supports that stuck out above the metal sheeting or the palm fronds that made up most of the fences. Through gaps left hanging open in the bent ridges of iron sheeting I could see the bare, trodden earth of the compound yards and the loose swathes of colored cloth that hung over the open doorways of the small plastered houses. The path trailed through piles of rotting garbage, over the glistening slime of an open sewer. Spindly chickens scrabbled through the trash heaps for something edible. Near the open gates of the compounds small children picked over the rubbish with them. It was like the poorer areas I'd already seen at the edge of Banjul, but the trees, the sounds of the birds, somehow made it seem more open, less oppressive.

As I made my way along the path I saw only children. Everyone else was inside. I'd never felt anything like the heat. It seemed to be standing over the village on large, muscular legs and pressing down on it with its sweaty hands. It had swept through the village earlier in the day and driven the people into their rooms, into the shadows. If I did see someone at a distance they were hurrying, as if they were trying to get out of the sun before they were noticed. At the edge of a field a group of women had gathered in the shade, in their bright robes

looking like exotic birds perched in the low hanging limbs of the trees.
Their voices, too far from me to be more than a sound, were like a
light chattering of birds, and I had the feeling that if I came too close
they would burst into flight and disappear over the roofs of the village.

I couldn't walk as quickly as Musa with the recording equipment
hanging from my shoulders, and I struggled through the dust, shifting
the heavy bags from one side to the other. I could see that he'd stopped
under the roof of a shed and was waiting for me to catch up with him.
Under the layer of dust the earth was as hard as stone, reflecting the
heat back up into my face. He was also panting when I stopped beside
him in the patch of shade.

'It's too hot for you?' he asked, out of breath.

I dropped the bags against a packing crate. 'Yes, it's too hot for me.'

'Look at me,' he said, wiping his face with his sleeve. 'I get hot when
I must walk out in the daytime. All people get hot.' He gestured
toward a narrow opening between the rows of fences. 'But it isn't so
far to go to the jali's compound. In a moment we can be there.'

I stood beside him catching my breath, looking around at the village.
It was wretchedly poor, but despite this there was a feeling of order
and care in the compounds. The earth of the yards had been swept with
brooms made of bundles of twigs; there were lines of clothes drying in
the sun. Beside many doorways there were digging tools and battered
water pans that the women used in their small vegetable gardens.

Musa looked at me questioningly, motioning toward the path. I
hitched the bags onto my shoulders again and squinted into the glare.
'We go on now,' he said, 'It is only a little way still to go.'

The jali's compound was behind a fence made of thatched palm fronds.
Three small buildings covered with light stucco, a packed earth yard, a
few large trees noisy with birds. A woman in a loose, brightly dyed
robe came to a doorway. She listened to Musa, tying her robe tighter.
The jali is with a neighbor, she told him, she'll send a boy for him, he'll
come soon. She pulled a low platform out of the sun and set it up in the
shade under the trees, then she slipped into the house and came out
again with a bowl of oranges. We each took one to suck. They were
greenish, filled with seeds, bitter-sweet, hot, the rind stinging the
tongue. Lying back on the platform, staring up into the matted leaves

as the dust drifted through them, I felt as if I'd begun moving, drifting through a wavering sea of distant sounds.

I already had some idea of the importance of the Mandingo jalis to their own societies. One reason for this, certainly, was that none of the African tribes had developed a written language. After the prolonged religious wars before the period of European colonization there was some use of Arabic, but throughout large areas there was no way to write anything down. Within every culture, however, there is a need to maintain a continuity from the past, and in the West African societies the role of the historian had been taken over by the singer-historians who were known as griots. Their position corresponded roughly to that of the bards or the skalds of medieval Europe, and when the first European travelers met the griots they were attached to the houses of kings or important local chieftans. A collection of travel writings published in London in 1745, *Green's Collection of Voyages*, has a number of references to the griots.

> Of the role of the musician in the society there seems to be considerable agreement, although there are differences in the name. 'Those who play on the instruments are persons of a very singular character, and seem to be their poets as well as musicians, not unlike the Bards among the Irish and the ancient Britons. All the French authors who describe the countries of the Jalofs and the Fulis call them *Guiriots*, but Jobson gives them the name of Juddies, which he interprets fiddlers. Perhaps the former is the Jalof and Fuli name, the latter the Mandindo.'
>
> The traveler Bardot says the Guiriot in the language of the Negroes toward the Sanaga, signifies Buffoon, and that they are a sort of syncophant. 'The Kings and great men in the country keep each of them two or more of these Guiriots to divert them and entertain foreigners on occasion.'*

The tribes which the account mentions are now called the Wollof and the Fula, and the French writers used their own word to describe the musicians. The word for singer in Fula is 'jelefo' and in Wollof the word is 'katt'. The account goes on to quote Jobson on the ambiguous position of the griots in the African societies, something that carried over into the attitudes toward the singers in the societies which the Africans built up in the United States and the Caribbean.

> The fiddlers (guiriots) are reckoned rich, and their wives have more crystal, blue stones, and beads about them than the king's wives ... and

* Notes to *The Griots*, New York, Folkways Records and Service Corp., 1975.

it is remarkable that after all this fondness of the people for music, and yet the Musician is held in great contempt and is denied their common rite of Burial, instead of which the Corpse is set upright in a hollow tree and left there to rot. The reason they give for this treatment is that these cantators have a familiar converse with their Devil, Ho-Re.*

More modern writers have also been critical of the griots, but for different reasons. Although their role, in part, is to relate the history of their people, an historian working in the Gambia basin, Charlotte A. Quinn didn't find that they were of much use to her. As she said when she listed the informants who had given her the most information,

An omission from the list of informants which is perhaps obvious to the reader is that of praise-singers, or *griots*, whose profession it is to collect bardic tales, songs, and poems which honor their patrons and vilify their sponsors' enemies. A fascinating study in themselves, the griots' tales collected during 1965 proved to be less valuable for the history of Gambian Mandingo society than the traditions and memories of nonprofessional informants whose livelihood was not dependent on the aesthetic or hortatory virtues of their presentation.**

It was one of these singers I was waiting to meet as I lay back on the platform staring up into the curtain of leaves over me.

After a thirty-minute wait the jali came into the compound. He was an older looking man in his late thirties, wearing a long blue robe that swept down from his shoulders. He had an air of importance, his face heavy and broad, his skin a dark, smooth black. He walked slowly, with a heavy limp. Musa had told me that he had only one leg and that the other was artificial. He had fallen from a tree as a boy when he was gathering coconuts. He called out to people in the buildings as he came across the compound yard, brushing flies away from his face with a large hand. Faces appeared at doorways, women abruptly wrapping themselves in skirts and blouses, pulling on turbans, all of the cloth richly colored in a tie-dye process that's characteristic of The Gambia. It was this bright cloth plumage which had given the women under the trees the look of vividly colored birds.

The jali shook hands and led us to his building, a stucco room with two doorways opening into a corner of the compound. His name was Nyama Suso, but he was usually called Jali Nyama by the people in the village; 'Nyama the singer'. He settled into a battered wooden chair

---

* *The Griots*
** Charlotte A. Quinn, *Mandingo Kingdoms of the Senegambia* (Evanston, Illinois: Northwestern University Press, 1972), p. xvii.

beside the sagging bed that almost filled the room. He laughed apologetically, 'I have to be paid for my songs. I have only my kora to take care of the people in my compound, and it takes so much to buy a sack of rice today. I can't walk so I must play'. He spoke English though it was heavily accented and obviously uncomfortable for him. Nine people lived in his compound; his wives, children and relatives. In the rainy season the young men work in the fields, but when it's been dry for months there's nothing for them to do. In this season they are as dependent on him as the women.

His accompanying instrument, the kora, was in a corner behind his chair. It was made out of a large, dried gourd shell – a calabash. The calabash had been cut roughly in half and the larger half became the sound box of the instrument. A long pole was pushed through the sides of the gourd. A short nub of the pole protruded from the bottom of the instrument and a two and a half foot length of the pole stuck out of the top. The opening of the gourd was covered with a thin goat-skin fitted to the sides with round upholstery tacks. At the bottom of the kora twenty-one plastic strings were attached to a ring that was lashed to the nub of the pole. The strings were stretched over a pyramid shaped wooden bridge that sat on the skin, tied to the long end of the pole with thin leather straps. The kora was tuned by sliding the leather straps up and down the pole, and the tuning was difficult since any change in a string altered the tension on all of them.

The strings of the kora at one time were made of sinew, but now they're cut from lengths of plastic fishing line and the sound is light and silvery; harp-like in character. Two smaller sticks are set into the top of the calabash, one on either side of the strings. The jali holds the kora with these two sticks, setting the instrument on his lap with the strings, the bridge, and the skin head toward him, the long stick of the instrument's neck projecting above the brown mottled shape of the calabash as if he were pointing it at someone. Jali Nyama held it with the last three fingers of each hand curled around the small sticks, leaving the thumbs and forefingers free to pick the strings, much as many guitarists in the southern states pick with thumb and forefinger.

He played a long, highly ornamented introduction; then began singing. The music was strongly expressive, a mixture of recitation and song. At times he told part of a story, then intermingled the narrative with comments and praises for the great men mentioned in the song.

The accompaniment he played on the kora was a repetitive, highly rhythmic figure that was light in texture and contrasted brilliantly with the dark tone of his voice. The structure of the song seemed to be built more on extended melodic phrases than it did on recurring verse patterns and I could hear sudden changes of mood in the tone and timbre of the voice. It was a technically exciting, and at the same time complex and demanding musical style.

At first I was surprised at how little the music sounded like the blues. The busy, running accompaniment figure in the kora had no definite points of stress accent. I couldn't tap my foot to the rhythm the way I could with a blues. There were no harmonies, none of the melodic figures that set the blues apart. I couldn't follow the verses; since he was singing in Mandingo, I couldn't even follow the words. But at the same time so much of the mood and style had overtones of something I had heard before. I had the uncanny feeling that I was hearing one of the early blues men, only now he was singing a different style of song. The vocal timbres, the shaping of the melody, the rhythmic openness of the singing all seemed to be directly related to the blues. I found myself swept up into the music. I was conscious that there was so much I didn't immediately understand about the style; things I would have to study when I wasn't involved with recording machines and microphones, but I also felt I had taken a first step toward understanding a little more of the musical background that I'd come to Africa to find.

I was the only one listening who didn't know the stories. The others had heard them so often that the comments and the skill in the accompaniment interested them as much as the songs themselves. He began another piece, this one in a sombre minor mode, and as he played the little accompaniment pattern over and over again he snapped a finger against one of the smaller sticks to emphasize the rhythm. Musa leaned over to tell me that it was called 'Chedo', or 'Khedo', as he pronounced it. I could hear a new, running instrumental figure between two of the verses. 'That is the queen's horses, as the soldiers ride into battle', he whispered.

'Chedo' is a classic of the Mandingo griot repertoire, and every singer has his own version of it. Nothing like its range of history or depth of expression made its way into Afro-American music. The word, in Fula, means Mandingo, and it describes the beginnings of the religious wars which led to the destruction of the Mandingo kingdom in the 19th Century, the war that the griots describe as 'the war to end war'. The war began as a squabble between the two tribes near the Mandingo capital of Kabo. As the song opens, the Fula warriors warn the Mandingo warriors of the Sanneh and Manneh families not to destroy the millet crop – the 'coos'. As with all griot narratives, Jali Nyama wove his own comments, moral judgements and isolated poetic images into it. A line like 'The bees have gotten into the wine ...' he said later meant that the warriors were coming to the battle they loved so well. The text of his 'Chedo', as Musa translated it later for me, was,

> Oh Chedo,
> Don't finish the coos,
> Don't finish the coos, you Sannehs and Mannehs.
>
> You people listening to me,
> War is not good, it is filled with death.
> Men lie dead without burial, friends kill each other,
> they see friends dying.
> You people don't know, Kabo is filled with warriors,
> the Sannehs and Mannehs.
> Who is the king in Kabo?
> The king is Janke Wali.
>
> Listen to Sani Bakari coming, the war is going badly,
> Listen to Sani Bakari standing up, ready to fight again.
>
> With love there must be trust,
> if you love someone they must be able to trust you.
> Knowing someone also brings sorrow.
> Now I love men who refuse me things and go on refusing.
>
> Oh, this world,
> many things have gone and passed,
> the world wasn't made today and it won't end today.
>
> All these things happened in the reign of Janke Wali.
> Oh grand Janke Wali, and Malang Bulefema, together with
> Yunkamandu, Hari Nimang, Lambi Nimang, Teremang Nimang,
> Kuntu Kuntu, Nimangolu.
> If you hear the word 'Nyancho' it means Sanneh and Manneh,
> the word 'koringolu' means Sonko and Sanyang.

The bees have gotten into the wine,
these that eat good meat and drink good wine ...

Hear the cries of a lazy woman who is saying 'The birds
are eating all my rice, I'll have to look for another
place to go'.

You don't know what it was like the day they were crying
for Malung to come out and fight.
It was a fierce, fearful day.
'Yungkamadu, come out and fight.'

You men who are ready to die today,
you must come out and meet the other warriors.

Days like these were never good.
The wars in Kabo were very fierce.
Those were the days of killing.

'Oh uncle, we don't want to be slaves to the Fulas'.

Quarreling every day ends love.
Oh, this world
the world that wasn't made today and won't end today. ...

People had begun to collect in the doorway and in the shade of the compound yard. Men slipped in the half-open gate and sat on the floor in front of us. Jali Nyama nodded to them as he sang, but there was no applause, no overt response. His narratives involved them completely since it was their own past he was singing about. The names he included in the songs were often the family names of people who lived in the village. The music wasn't a kind of proto-blues. The alternation of narration and comment, the rhythms themselves, were too different to relate to the verse forms of the blues, but the *role* of the griot was certainly the same as that of the blues man in a village in the South.

An hour passed. He sang one of the histories of the village families which are a griot's stock in trade. It was these narratives that became increasingly important for them as their support from local kings and warriors and rich merchants dwindled. The people of the villages now hire the griots to sing about their own families at festivals and family gatherings. When it was finished Jali Nyama played a last florid instrumental passage, leaned his kora back in its corner, and sat fanning himself with a printed blue cotton handkerchief. 'Do you like my songs?' he asked. Certainly. 'But why do you come to listen to the griots?' I tried to say something about the relationship I was trying to trace between the two kinds of music and the two societies, the one African, the other Afro-American. There was a silence in the small room. Finally one of the men who had come in as Jali Nyama was singing asked carefully, 'It was so many years ago. Haven't you come too late?' It was so many years ago, but I hadn't come too late.

The day had become cooler. There were shadows in the corner of the room and through the doorway I could see the sun hanging in a red streak of cloud over the low roofs of the houses. Jali Nyama pulled himself out of the battered chair and walked slowly with me across the compound and into the village. As the heat had seeped out of the dust-filled air the village had come to life again. The rutted pathways which had been empty earlier had filled with people who jostled past each other calling out greetings over their shoulders. Musa Camara had to go back to his own compound in a new area of the village and he hurried away. Jali Nyama and I went from street to street, the 'streets' themselves only rutted and pitted uneven dirt stretches between the lines of corrugated iron fencing. Some of the passageways were trampled down enough for cars to push through, lurching and bleating with horns that sounded as helpless as the bleating of the young goats who ran nervously away from them.

The air was filled with noises, but they were small in dimension. Men were hammering on a wheel, birds were whistling from the trees, women's voices were raised in greetings. It was like the restless movements in a bush when it is momentarily filled with a small flock of birds. For me it was new and fascinating, to Jali Nyama it was only a part of his everyday life. We came to a small opening in the center of the village, a clearing with a small open-sided building where children sat repeating verses from the Koran. Above it towered a tree that covered the compounds close by with its shade and filled their yards with dropping leaves and bark. He pointed toward its massive, entwined trunk and said with a short laugh, 'I born in that tree's shadow. It hang there over me all my life. But see it's like the village, with everything coming all together. You see it's two trees inside each other − that one on the inside and then one on the outside where the other grew up in it. It all come together like that.'

As we went on he pointed to a long line of dilapidated fence, the top of the metal strips higher than my shoulder. 'You can see, starting from the other end of the path here to the tree, that's all one compound. One man have that, though sometimes if he have another wife he have another place to come to as well.'

'Were they always so big?' I asked, since the space enclosed in the fence seemed to be half the size of a football field and was filled with trees and small open buildings and a jumbled rubbish heap.

'They same big now. Just the same. But now they don't have so many people. When I grew up people used to have big compounds. You know they used to have more than fifty people in one compound, more than sixty people in one compound, in some nearly a hundred people all living together.' He shook his head. 'It isn't so easy all the time living together. Sometimes a man must have a small space he can go to, to be with himself.' Then he laughed again. 'I don't know how it is in your country, but here in Africa when you come home with a new wife then your old wife she angry for a time.'

I told him that it was also difficult in my country when you brought a new wife home to your old wife. Did he take care of everything in the compound?

'I must do it all. Each man who is head of his compound must do it like that, only in my compound it is just one, just me that must do everything to get the money. I'm doing everything to get the food, to get the market money and so forth. If anybody in the compound have a job they bring me part of the money but I must do it all. And every morning the women come to see me and say, "Well, we're going to the market," so I give them what I have to give them so they can buy what they need, and sometimes we talk and talk a long time because they want to get the money from me, and I say why do you need the money and they say because I must have it. I don't know if you have the same problem in your country with your wives.'

Just outside the open gate of a compound the women were sitting around a bucket of water peeling roots and dropping the slippery white bits into the bucket to be cooked for dinner. There was a laughing conversation with the Jali as we passed. He spoke to them in two or three languages, saying the same thing in each, or I had the feeling, at least, that he said the same thing since they all giggled the same way. They were tall, handsome women, in loose blouses and lengths of colored skirt material that went down to their ankles. Most of them wore turbans, but one or two had their heads bare and I could see the elaborate braiding that pulled the hair into even rows. There were Mandingo, Fula and a Serrehule woman, her face marked with tribal scars.

'Before it was all the same people in Bakau,' Jali Nyama said as he limped along the path. 'Then it was Fula and Mandingo' – which he pronounced 'Mandinka' – 'then it was all mixed up. Like that big tree in the middle. Now we have everybody here and if you see a Jola you speak to him in Jola and if you see a Fula you speak to him in Fula. Everybody must get along together now.'

But how could he as a griot still be part of village life when it was changing all around him? How could he know enough about the new people who came into the village to be able to sing about them?

'I know it already, before they come.' He seemed surprised that I needed to ask. 'I know all the names of the people because that is my job as a jali, a jaliba' – jaliba means important singer – 'I must know the history of the families and I must know how your great-grandfather and your father come down to you. I learn all of this because we, my family, we seven generations of musicians here. We aren't just people who come after, we are the beginning of the griots here. You see, we *know* it.'

Could they add new things to the song about a name? 'We do it when anybody ask us. We hear about something that happened in the family many years ago and we put it into the song. People come to us and they say this is so and so – my ancestor he did this or he did that – he did this great thing or this terrible thing happened to him and they say to us can you put it in a song. We must do it because it is our job and they give us money.'

How long did it take to work something into one of the griot songs? Jali Nyama shrugged. 'Two days. Three days. We think about what it is we will sing and then we practise it and then we have it ready.'

We had come close to the market place and there was a sound of voices and the noise of children playing a game of soccer with a half-filled, tattered ball on a patch of bare ground strewn with ashes. On the other side of it I could see a taxi parked under a tree. It would take me back to Banjul. We stood talking for a last moment.

'Do you know too much about people sometimes?' I asked. 'Yes. *Yes*,' he answered, his strong face broadening with laughter again. 'We know too much about everybody. But we don't tell, you know. That isn't what our job is.' As I sat in the noisy cab rattling back toward Banjul the muted sounds of the village still filled my ears.

3

'I Can Tell You The History of Everything'

I was staying in a simple hotel close to the river in Banjul, with a sitting room and bedroom that led out to a small balcony which was four flights above the town's ferry landing. At the other side of the room was a small kitchen. There was no food in the hotel except for bread and eggs which were left inside my door every morning. I ate dinner in the small restaurants on the side streets and went to the market place every morning to get something for lunch or to take with me out into the countryside. No matter how early I awoke there were already people hurrying along the street and there was a murmur of voices around me as I followed them to the market through the pale, streaming light.

The high plaster walls surrounding the market were broken only with two small gates opening to the street, but behind the walls' white painted stillness there was a warren of booths selling lengths of printed cloth, plastic shoes, enameled pans, cooking utensils, combs, elastic, leather, canned goods, and soap. Behind them, in the shadowy recesses of the market, cement stalls piled with fruit, vegetables, spices. Women were everywhere. Their sweeping robes gathered up under one armpit, they bent over gnarled pans of peppers, onions and tomatoes piled up in small careful pyramids. In an open area against the market's back wall women were standing at stained cement troughs slicing bits of meat into smoke blackened pans. The air was choked with the pungent smells of cooking as men crowded around open fires to buy fried meat and thin loaves of bread. Some were in European clothes; mingled with them were men from the desert tribes, in their loose white trousers and blue burnooses. Their clothes were creased and dirty, stained with dark rings of sweat. Only the adolescent boys from

Banjul, in shorts and washed tee shirts, looked as if they'd slept under shelter the night before.

The market place was always so busy and so much went on inside its crowded walls that it seemed to me that I must see new things in it every day, but I soon realized that it was always the same, morning after morning. The same smells, the same crowd of half-awake men around the cooking food, the same women with their little heaped stocks of fruits and vegetables. Across the street from the market, against the building fronts, much buying and selling was also going on along the sidewalk. Dyed cloth, piles of sandals, trays of watches and sunglasses held on laps, the sellers squatting on pieces of cardboard dragged back against the walls of the buildings. There was jostling and pushing just as there was across the street in the market, but I didn't feel that anyone had any animosities toward anyone else.

The men didn't say anything to the women in native robes, but they called after the occasional woman swaggering past in European clothes and straightened hair. 'Come over to me sweetheart, come over to me now. I treat you right'. 'Look at me, darling, I'm a bad man. I'm a bad man. You try me and see'. For prostitutes the treatment is the same the world over.

The mouth of the Gambia River at Banjul gapes into the Atlantic like a beached fish, its sides as flat and dull as the fish's scales when it's lain out in the sun. Banjul lines the south bank with its stucco buildings, palm trees and lines of fishing boats pulled up on the sand. On the north shore is the low, white painted ruin of an old British fort and the straggling buildings of a river village. When the British first established their trading concession in the area, the store was twenty miles upstream on a small island in the center of the river. The small fort there had been destroyed by the French in 1703, but when the British decided to patrol the coast in an effort to end the slave trade, the Secretary of State, Lord Bathurst, decided to build a new fort on the site, or somewhere close by. The work party sent out by the governor of Senegal, Charles MacCarthy, decided that it would be more effective to control the river from its mouth and in 1806 the new fort was set up on the sand bar which became the site of the settlement then called Bathurst.

Victorian travelers, who seemed to get everywhere, also made their way to the settlement. Captain J.F. Napier Hewett, describing it in 1862, was impressed with the gleaming sand of the beaches as his ship sailed into the mouth of the river, but everything after that was downhill.

> ... Though the bright sand was pleasing to the eye at distant view, it was far from agreeable when near, for the whole island and the roads of Bathurst consist of sand knee-deep, and burning like hot ashes, which, when the wind blew, was whirled in clouds into the eyes, nose, and mouth; its glare dazzled the vision; and its depth was such as to require severe struggles in progress. The verdant appearance of the town, as seen from the river, is likewise deceptive, the land, as far as the eye can reach, being a sandy waste, devoid of timber or shrubs, the only attempt at vegetation the row of caoutchouc trees which, as I have mentioned, front the water; a few cocoa-nut and palm trees, a few scrubby paw-paw trees, some willows, bananas, Oleanders, Quayves, and Barbadoes Pride ... in one quarter of the town, where several houses adjoin one another, the footway is like the Colonnade under the Opera, Haymarket, minus the glittering shops; for although these exist here also, such as they are, are dirty and dusty, and emit intolerable odours, mingled with effluvia emanating from the stables, which are generally situated in the basement story. But the traveler is almost unable to notice or feel interested in anything, his whole energies being directed toward wading through the sand, endeavouring to exclude the noisome effluvia which everywhere assails his nostrils, and if he is about to undergo a sojourn, his mind is engrossed in bewailing the hardship of his lot. Never shall I forget this my first experience of the amenities of Gambia, and the horrors of the walk! In addition to the evils above enumerated, the heat, although the hour was only 10 a.m., was intolerable, and made me feel sick and giddy; the wind, when breathing across the face of a whitewashed wall, blew fiery and suffocating, like the air from a furnace ...*

For Captain Hewett, and other travelers, Bathurst didn't, as they would have put it, improve upon further acquaintance. When the British leased the land from a local chieftain in 1806 it was uninhabited simply because it was uninhabitable. It was flat, sandy, barren, hot and pestilent, but within a few years it had become the home of several hundred Nigerian Yoruba and Ibos who had been freed from seized slave ships, and three or four thousand people from the tribes of the

---

* Captain J.F. Napier Hewett, *European Settlements on the West Coast of Africa* (Reprint of 1862 Edition, New York: Negro Universities Press, 1969), p. 65.

surrounding countryside. The European population was small and desperate, and at any given period more of them were in the settlement's cemetery than there were in Bathurst itself. The cemetery was along the beach behind one of the headlands, and during occasional periods of high water the markers were obliterated, and the newly arriving governor often had difficulty locating the grave of his predecessor.

But over the years some of the swamp was filled in, the streets paved, trees and bushes planted, and the settlement began to have the character of an ordinary British colonial city, with a cluster of heavy, white-painted government buildings, a parade ground, and rough squares of African compounds stretching behind the one street of small, dark shops. The filling still goes on away from the center of Banjul, and at the edges of the mangrove swamp there are strings of compounds along the straggling roads, like tendrils of vines stretching out to plant new roots.

A week after I'd been with Jali Suso I heard again from Musa Camara. Musa had a small salary from his job with the government radio service, but he was also in need of money so that he could get married. The difficulty wasn't so much that he needed money for them to live on – his wife would simply move into the small compound Musa shared with his two sisters – he had to scrape up the money to 'buy' his wife from her family. It was still called a 'bride price,' and at some point in time it had a more ceremonial aspect, but in modern Banjul it was largely a cash transaction, since Musa couldn't be expected to offer cows, the traditional gift item. Virgins cost considerably more than women who had been married, but there was a bride price for any marriageable woman. Jali Suso was also saving money for a new wife, but since the woman he was interested in was divorced and in her thirties her price was only fifteen pounds. For something as important as this the reckoning was still done in British currency. Musa's bride cost considerably more, and I paid him every time he took me to a musician, as well as for his work doing rough translations of the material for me. He had left a note under my door telling me that one of the most important of The Gambia's Mandingo griots had come in from his village in the bush and that he would see me in his compound in Banjul.

Musa had asked me to meet him at the singer's compound in the morning; so after I'd finished cooking eggs on my sputtering stove I put the dishes in the sink and began walking across Banjul. I was getting used to the people and the noise of the streets, but I still walked slowly, savouring the atmosphere when I got away from the shopping area and came into the crowded compound areas. I kept out of the sun by staying close to the walls of the one-storey buildings or the iron fences of the compounds. A few of the buildings were stucco, the rest built of corrugated iron and plastered poles. There was the usual stench from the open sewers that lined the edge of the houses in a long black maw. Women clustered at the pumps, but there was none of the light exchange I'd heard in Bakau. The women didn't look at each other, no one talked. They only waited patiently with their jars and buckets. The walls of the houses were backed up against the street, the windows opened, the curtains pulled back. I could see small rooms crowded with old bedsteads and stained mattresses. In one window the brass pinnacle of the bed, and in the next a dangling model of the old fishing boats that are built along the coast. In the next window a man standing at a dresser in his underwear, moving cans, bottles, pictures out of the way as he searched for something. He looked up as a woman came in the doorway. Two bare feet protruded on either side of her wrapped waist – a baby tied against her back in the folds of her robe, its face staring round-eyed at me through the window.

The singer's compound was at the end of a street covered with broken bits of sea shell. Beyond the rattling walls of his fence, the green arms of the mangroves thrust down into the current of dark brown water streaming past them. The compound was the usual picked-over space of dry earth with a line of small rooms in a long building on one side of it. Wooden seats had been set out beside the doorways and long trailing curtains fluttered like green winged moths against the white-washed walls. Musa was early and was waiting for me outside the compound fence. We shook hands and went inside the gate. The women pounding millet hesitated, the thin wooden pestles suspended over worn wooden mortars cut from tree trunks. They made an effort to cover bare breasts, not because of any shyness, but unsure of what a foreigner would think of their nakedness. As we walked past them the rhythmic thud of the pounding picked up again, the bare breasts shook in the sunlight, the women's eyes stared shyly up at us from lowered faces.

Musa introduced me to the heavy, brown-robed man coming toward us across the compound. He was Alhaji Fabala Kanuteh, one of the most important of the Mandingo griots, one of the two singers employed as griots by the President of The Gambia. When he was three he had been taken to his grandfather's house at Manding, in the interior and had stayed there for twenty-four years learning the songs and the narratives of Mandingo history. He spoke a little English, but he was guarded. 'I would not come except this man ask me.' When he finished singing for me he was to go on to the Presidential Palace to discuss arrangements for the festival to honor The Gambia's nine years of independence the following month. 'It isn't because you pay me that I will sing for you, but I would like to come to your country as the representative of the Mandingo people.' 'Alhaji' meant that he had made the pilgrimage to Mecca, and even though he was a singer, a 'jali', like Nyama Suso, he was so imposing I couldn't address him as anything else but Alhaji.

The Mandingo griots have two instruments. One is the kora that Jali Nyama played. It is considered a 'newer' instrument. The older instrument is a small balafon, a handmade wooden xylopone. The balafon used by the griots is called the balanjie. It's small enough for a singer to carry with him as he walks from village to village. The nineteen 'keys' are cut from a hard, reddish wood, and they're laid on a frame of sticks held together with cord lashings. A dried calabash suspended below each key gives the sound more resonance. Walking on ahead, Alhaji Fabala led us to one of the rooms, sat impassively on the floor on a woven mat and pulled his balafon in front of him against his bare feet.

It was a corner room in the compound with printed cloth curtains in the doorway. The room was filled with the usual sagging double bed, covered with a bright blue and yellow spread. Homemade wooden chairs had been pushed back against chipped plaster walls. Across the room from me the wall was filled with pictures, photographs of family and friends set in frames made of glass window panes painted with flower decorations. Alhaji Fabala began to try different patterns on the balafon, playing with thin wooden mallets. The sound was low and quiet, as dry as the dust of the compound yard. He finished with a flurrying run up the keys, his mood changing. He shifted his shoulders a little, pulled his robe back from his feet. He looked over at me and said slowly, 'Playing is my job'.

The first 'song' was a long recitation about the early life of Almami Samory Touré, 'a king who had many slaves'. He had fought against the Europeans with some success from 1882 to 1898 and he was still an inspiring figure to many people in West Africa, among them his grandson Sekou Touré, the president of Guinea. Alhaji Fabala's voice was slow, almost meditative. It was light in tone, but he told the story so convincingly – with so much elaborate variation in phrase and rhythm that I found myself listening to every word, even though I couldn't understand what he was saying. The recitation was interrupted from time to time with scurrying passages on the balafon, the small mallets clattering up and down the keys. Occasionally he half sang, half hummed a melody with a series of set phrases praising famous men. While he was resting his voice in these interludes Musa leaned over to where I was sitting on the floor and whispered bits of the story in my ear. With a last flourish Alhaji Fabala played an ascending run on the balafon and leaned back against the bed, obviously satisfied with his performance. I became conscious that the sounds of the compound had gone on without interruption. Chickens were still squawking, children were still shouting, women were still pounding millet. I'd been listening so intently I hadn't noticed.

The accompaniment he played on the balafon was a simple rhythmic figure that repeated itself over and over, with the occasional flurries of notes to mark sections of the story. He played softly to keep from drowning out his voice, half tapping, half touching the keys with the mallets. Again, as with the music of Jali Nyama Suso I felt so close to the beginning of the blues, but with the narratives of Alhaji Fabala I was even further back in time. The things he was reciting were too important to make into a song. This kind of careful telling was the only way he could present the story to me. It is less complicated to sing about the relatively simple emotional situations of the blues.

I asked him what he could tell me about the Europeans – about the first meetings with them. He half-smiled and shrugged. 'I can tell you the history of everything, Africa, India, China, everything. But you must come when you have time to listen'. He looked thoughtful and tapped the balafon with a stick. 'The Europeans? It is a hard song to do and it goes on for a day and a half. I don't sing it often'.

The song was about the Mandingo kings who collected slaves to sell to the Portuguese. It was the same kind of recitation as the first song he'd performed, meditative and careful, the instrument following with its light, cupped tones. It was almost like pieces of wood were hanging from strings in the doorway and swaying against each other in the breeze. Again, Musa leaned over to tell me what the song was about in the sections of praising which alternated with the verses of the song itself, but I could feel that Musa was also listening more intensely than before. It was obviously something he hadn't heard before. I could hear words I knew myself – 'mansa,' the word for king, 'jonga,' the word for slave – the names of the places along the river – then 'America'. I was sure that listening to the first chanted histories thousands of years before had been the same kind of experience as I was having in Alhaji Fabala's cramped room.

His song described the first meetings with the Portuguese and the first sales of slaves to them by the Mandingo king Musa Molo. The Portuguese had then sold them to the Dutch, who in 1619 had brought them to 'America'. It was a Dutch ship that had brought the first shipment of slaves to the English colony in Virginia; so it could have been this first group of slaves that I was hearing about. Musa Molo was so pleased with the first sales that he ordered his chieftians to build something to keep the slaves in while they waited for the Portuguese to come back. What they built was a 'slaf house', as Alhaji Fabala called it, at a place called Jang Jang Bure.

The song ended. I could hear the words 'Portuguese', 'America', and then 'American Negro'. He finished with another rattling flourish on the balafon and the room fell silent. Musa stood up excitedly and reached into his pocket. 'You must have my shilling', he said, giving him the ceremonial payment for an especially moving performance.

Alhaji Fabala gravely took the money, listened to my efforts to compliment him, and shook his robe down from his shoulders. 'That was from my father's father and his father's father's,' he said finally. Outside the doorway the sounds began again and the curtain blew against my face. I was conscious that time had passed and the heat of the day waited for me in the glare of the yard.

'The place is still there, where they kept the slaves', Alhaji Fabala said to me when we walked toward the gates of the compound. The women in the yard, no longer embarrassed and suddenly openly curious, straightened up and looked at us, the millet beaters in their hands, their bodies shining with perspiration. 'The place where they kept the slaves. It is still there up the river'.

'Yes, I know of it too', Musa, said. 'My father has seen it'. It was on the Gambia River at a place called Georgetown or Jang Jang Bure. There was some uncertainty over the name. The best way to get there was to ride one of the small covered trucks that waited for passengers on the side streets of Banjul.

Even though we'd been in the shaded room Alhaji Fabala was also sweating, and he wiped his face as he talked, using his large handkerchief with abrupt gestures like a man swatting flies. 'Jang Jang Bure', he said again. 'The slave house is there. If you want to know about slave times you go to that place'.

Musa and I had agreed to have dinner together when the day had become cooler, and he came to the door of the hotel after dark. He had grown up in a small town up the river, but he had already adapted himself to the life of the city. He was in a red shirt, with striped red and white trousers, the colors a vivid contrast to his dark, almost black skin. We crossed the street to one of the ramshackle little stands so he could get some cigarets, and then walked through the streets looking for something to eat.

'We must eat African food, I think', he said as a question. I answered yes.

'European food, you know, after African food it doesn't have any taste. I have to eat it sometime. French food and English food. But they don't know how to do it. It doesn't have any spices. When you get finished you don't think you've had anything to eat. That's the truth'.

As we walked, the night air hummed with some of the sounds of a city — cars passing, footsteps rattling on the pavement — but in the back streets the mood was that of a small village. Men sat talking and smoking in groups at the corners, light streamed from the vendors' stalls, from the lanterns hanging from nails on the poles. In the compounds' dark yards I could see the bright red points of charcoal fires and the moving shapes of the women crossing back and forth in their endless work. Sounds of spoons clanking against cooking pans, of dry trees rattling over our heads.

The eating place was in the second story of a square wooden building that the British had built as a social club. The boards were peeling and dull, the sign above the battered door almost too faint to read. It was dark inside. Only a flutter of light from the juke box against the wall, from small colored bulbs on old advertising signs behind the bar. Men were sitting in the semi-darkness with bottles of beer, the dark skin of faces and arms difficult to see in the dimness. It could have been one of the bars I was used to on Chicago's South Side, except that it was quieter, no one was watching me, and the smells in the air eddying through the half opened, sagging louvres had a soft, melancholy sweetness. It was as if the night outside was choked with flowers pressing themselves against the board walls.

The room upstairs was empty. A kitchen had been built at one end of it years before, and the boards were glazed with cracked paint and cooking grease. There were some tables set out in the room, chairs pushed against them. The walls had been painted with 'scenes' at one point, boats on the river, musical instruments, tribal masks. The walls were so darkened and scarred that they had become artifacts in themselves. To get something to eat you waited at a window cut into the wooden partition back at the kitchen. The menu was written on a small blackboard with a piece of chalk, cooked meat and rice was thirty cents. The woman, perspiring over the two-burner butane stove, called downstairs for beer. The food was raw and strong, the meat cooked with bits of fresh pepper. It was strongly flavoured in a way that European food never is. We clattered spoons on metal plates. I needed beer to help down the peppers, even though it wasn't the hottest African food I'd eaten. Musa laughed at me, pushed his plate away, and leaned back in his blue enameled wooden chair.

'The food's still strong for you?'

'It is strong,' I had to admit, 'but I like it.'

He smiled again, his face thin and young, his strong teeth gleaming as he laughed.

'So what have you learned now?'

'About what?'

'About the things you came to find out. About the songs of the jali and the old days and the time of the slaves.'

I shook my head. 'I don't know. When I came I thought I knew so much.' Then I asked suddenly, 'What about you? You never say what you think of the old days that the jali sings about.'

Musa shrugged.

'We don't think about it so much, that's the truth. It was so long ago. It isn't only you who wants to know. Sometimes we meet Americans, black people who come from Africa, and they try to talk to us about it. But what can I tell them? I can only tell them what I know as a Fula.'

I considered what he was saying, half listening to the noises of cars in the street, the rattling of palm fronds against the louvres outside the windows. The juke box was turned on downstairs. I always came back to the same point with the people I talked to in Africa. I couldn't use terms as general as 'African' or even 'West African'. I had to think in terms of tribes and tribal cultures. The strong, sudden smile again, his voice amused. 'Because the Fulas are great warriors. We sold the others.'

I had seen the rough census figures for the early slave trade; I had notes in the shoulder bag I'd taken with me. Few Fulas were sold. Of slaves taken from the Gambia basin they numbered less than one percent.

'But you don't think of the other tribes? The ones who were sold?' I persisted.

He shrugged. 'It was a time of wars. It was not a good time for anyone. People were sold. But they always did that in the wars. I only think as a Fula and it didn't happen to us. Instead of that I think about the wars and the stories of the warriors. You think too much about the other things.'

'But I should go to Jang Jang Bure?'

'There is something to see there. Where you want to go is the place where they kept the slaves. People say you can see the walls and the places where they had the chains. If that's what you want to do.'

The chairs rattled like sticks dropping on the wooden floor as we stood up. It was something I wanted to do. He had already begun talking about something else when we reached the corner, said goodnight, and I went back to the hotel through the empty streets.

4

A River Place

One of the positive aspects of traveling without any kind of plan is that you often don't know how you're going to get from one place to another. Occasionally you'll lose a day or two while you try to find out which truck or train or cart will get you where you want to go, but you'll usually find yourself traveling the way the people themselves do — which is always an absorbing experience even if it's sometimes a little uncomfortable.

The trucks that traveled into the interior were parked under a row of unkempt, bare trees in one of the city's districts of old plaster and wood compounds. There was one large building close by, a Victorian church, its stucco cornices faded and weathered, its pitched roof and leaded windows uneasily lifting tentative arms up over the straggling houses. The street itself was paved in the center, but the trucks were pulled off onto the dirt walkways between the paving and the black trench of the open sewer that ran close to the houses. It wasn't a deep sewer, and its smells were close to the surface, mingling with the scent of dirt and oil fumes from the trucks, the sweetish smells of rotting fruit, and the thin, gray drift from the charcoal fires. It was stifling hot under the trees. The drivers were stretched out in the covered spaces in the backs of the small, battered vehicles. They had added metal roofs to the trucks; there were wooden benches covered with thin, dirty padding running down the sides and dusty canvas side hangings. A low drone of music trickled from radios in the shadowy insides of the trucks, the sun streaked down the canvas hangings to the freight left in heaps beside the truck steps, waiting to be lifted on to roof luggage racks. Burlap bags, bursting suitcases tied with string, chickens thrusting nervous heads through the ribs of boxes, a small pig tied by one jerking leg to a rust flecked pole holding up the truck canopy. The helpers for the trucks sprawled against the trees on the dirt; usually these were younger men and boys in dirty, patched clothes, their eyes red from the dust, their bare feet and arms scarred from dragging boxes and crates and suitcases up and down the back of their trucks. They wore shorts, ragged tee shirts, rubbed with greasy hands from truck repairs, then wiped with the crusted dust of the road.

When would the trucks leave in the morning? Uncertainty. The helpers looked from one to another. English little help. What language did they speak? Drowsy voice from inside a truck. 'No time. We go when we have enough.' A driver had lifted his head, shading his eyes against the afternoon glare beyond the truck. Whispering among the helpers, one of them asking, uncertainly, where I was going. 'Jang Jang Bure.' The African name I'd been given by the Jali. No response from the boys under the trees. I tried the other name. 'Georgetown.' Heads nodded. 'We come to the river at Georgetown. You go across yourself.' It was the sleep-weighted voice of the driver in the truck's shadows. I called out my thanks and walked slowly back toward Banjul's main street.

In the morning I could feel a faint shift in the wind. It was scudding in off the ocean and it smelled of spray and sea birds and the debris washed up on the beaches. It was still cool under the trees where the shabby fleet of passenger trucks was parked. No one could tell me when the next one would leave, and each truck had its own helpers trying to talk people on to their vehicle. Travelers had begun to gather and women were moving along the sides of the trucks with nuts, fruit and bread on worn trays. It seemed completely confused and without order, but somehow the system did work in its own fashion. I had heard many people say that travel is impossibly chaotic in West Africa, but I found that the systems of getting from one place to another in the countryside were haphazard but also dependable in their own way. There were no schedules, but if you traveled as the Africans did – that is taking into consideration all the difficulties of the roadways and the condition of the trucks – it usually worked out. It was often uncomfortable, but West Africa isn't a country of luxuries, and the friendliness of the other travelers made up for much of the roughness of the roads. I had, after all, been living in a small town in Connecticut in the United States which had no public transportation of any kind. However raffish the system was here in Banjul, it was more advanced than what I had there in the United States, where I didn't have any way to travel at all.

One truck seemed a little nearer leaving than the others; so I climbed in, pushed my canvas bag under the bench, and waited. An hour passed. The sun grew hotter. The long hard wooden benches slowly filled around me. One of the first to follow me under the truck's canopy was a man in a long green shirt and a brocaded white cloth hat. He was carrying a shining new bicycle pump the way a British officer would have carried a swagger stick. Then two women followed with bundles of cloth and new cooking pans which they pushed under the bench. A boy in new denim shorts and a light jacket of the same material. He looked so out of place that I found myself staring at him. Men in white shirts and pressed slacks. An old man in a long brown robe and cap. Since we were in the city and there were trucks still to be filled the driver stopped at the legal limit painted on the outside of the cab: 11 passengers. Much noisy advice as we backed out, hands gesticulating, the helpers trying to move people out of the way. We turned into the street as the helpers, with a bursting run, caught up, pulled themselves up on the iron ladder and swung over the tailgate.

For the first hundred miles there was a black paved roadway that moved in small, humped undulations away from the coast. The ocean wind was left behind at the first villages, and after an hour it was hot, and the heat grew with each mile. Cattle ambled across the road, running only when they felt the truck's breath close to them. Goats, long-legged and thin, as nervously abrupt in their movements as dogs, scattered more easily, only the small white-faced baby goats staying at the edge of the road, bleating after the tails of their hurrying mothers. It was hard and uncomfortable on the unyielding benches, but the villages slipped past, and at about one in the afternoon, halfway on the journey, the truck pulled in to the corrugated iron shade beside a stucco building at a crossroads. We stood up, tired and cramped, stretching stiff arms and legs. We helped each other out of the back of the truck and went to get something to eat.

We'd come to a small crossroads village, with a gasoline pump and a line of huts beside the road. The building where we'd stopped seemed to be the only place to eat, and the only food was a simmering pan of spiced meat. People were sitting on their heels under the roof canopy eating boiled cassava, sucking on mottled green oranges, chewing handfuls of dried peanuts. I had bread which I'd put in my shoulder bag, and I sat in the shade chewing on the hard crust. A man with a wooden bowl filled with peanuts gave me a handful, and we ate peanuts together in a companionable silence. Other trucks were strung along the road like a straggling of goats. I could see the driver of one of them sitting behind a broken windshield, his face wrapped in a dark turban against the dust, as though he were still driving a camel instead of his dented truck.

We stayed at the crossroads only thirty minutes, but the sun was too hot for us to leave the shade so we remained close to the side of building. We were gathered by the truck when the driver came into the sunlight, rubbing his mouth with his sleeve. Two men had taken their bundles and were leaving us there. They turned and said short prayers for our safety and the people around me murmured the responses. I could see that the boy who had been dressed in the new denim shorts and jacket had changed to a loose blouse of faded cotton cloth. At first, when we'd settled back into the truck, I didn't understand why he'd done it. Then, a few moments after the truck had creaked away from the building I realized why he had been so careful. Just outside the village we turned onto a dirt road and a cloud of choking red dust suddenly billowed up from the road's pitted surface and swirled over us.

Despite the road's ruts and potholes, the driver rushed as fast as he could over it, as if he were trying to escape the cloud of dust behind us. But despite the wrenching, the tired lurching over the stones and troughs under the wheels, the dust seeped in, finding its way around the frayed edges of the canvas screen the driver's helper was holding closed with his bare feet as he tried to sleep. It streamed in along the openings in the truck's screened sides, under the low, stifling roof. It hung in the air around us, our teeth grating with it when we closed our mouths.

After a few hours of the dust all of us in the back of the truck became the same color. My white arm, touching the black arm beside me as we both grimly clung to a battered metal brace to keep from sliding, had darkened to a deep brown-red. The skin of his arm against mine had become the same darkish red from the dust, and our stiff lips were cracked with the same brown dryness when we tried to smile through the dimness. My straight light hair had become heavy and thickened with the dust, and it was the same color as the short, matted hair of the man sitting across from me, who was peeling roots, despite the truck's shaking, and passing small bits around to the rest of us.

The truck now careened unsteadily as it rattled through the countryside. We were overloaded. The driver had kept crowding new passengers in as we went through the small villages. Trucks and taxis going through isolated areas always got overcrowded. I didn't mind it because part of the reason the driver was crowding people in was to get them out of the heat. No one could say when the next truck might come along, and it might be even more crowded. He'd accumulated seventeen of us, along with two babies and a fifty pound bag of rice. Despite the importance of the road – it was the only one crossing the Gambia basin inside the country – there were only small, scattered villages alongside it. The huts were made of sticks and stuccoed earth, the compound areas screened in with woven reeds. Except for a few government cars using the road on official business, the occasional truck was the only vehicle that passed through most of the day. I still had a few inches of space left on the wooden bench, but I was wedged in between a nervous young man who kept trying to look out under the canvas sides and an overweight Mandingo woman in a flowing blue and white robe a few inches from me, that slowly darkened as I stared at it. Despite the dust, a Serrehule woman on the bench across from me was nursing a baby wrapped under her wrinkled shawl.

We had picked up the bag of rice under protest as we left a village where the driver had stopped to get some fruit. An old woman who had been waiting for a truck to stop since dawn hurried over to where we'd parked. Two of her sons followed her and they began arguing with the driver when he told her there was no more room. The driver, a thin, worried looking man with dark, scarred skin, his clothes dyed red with the road's dust, finally gave in, thinking it was only a thin old woman we'd added, and her sons helped lift her into the jammed space. We finally managed to make room for her near the opening at the back by shifting feet a few inches and sliding even closer together on the benches. The woman was chewing a nut, shifting it from one side of her mouth to another. As the driver pulled his door open she leaned out and began shouting, interrupting herself to spit out a stream of juice; then shouting again in a high, wheezing voice. It was at this point that the bag of rice appeared. One of her sons came around a mud wall dragging it after him. The driver stopped. The bag had to go on the truck with her. The driver protested vehemently, waving his arms in the son's impassive face. There was a prolonged argument. The woman went on shouting, spitting out juice every dozen words. She was obviously much more determined than the driver, who was trying ineffectually to ignore her and talk to the son, who kept his eyes on his mother's face. It had to go on the truck with us. We struggled to shift our feet again, lifted up bundles from the floor of the truck and held them on our laps. The Serrehule woman managed to get her belongings across her knees and rested the baby on top of the load. The sack of rice was shoved onto the floor and the old woman settled on it, her wrinkled face working as she chewed a fresh piece of nut and listened to the driver still arguing with her son. Her back was to us, and she hadn't turned around to look at us since the dispute had started. Finally, with a grinding sigh from the engine and a whining creak from the sagging springs we struggled back on the pitted surface of the road.

It was the sack of rice that finally brought us to a halt. We were too heavily loaded. As we swayed up a hill with all the lumbering grace of an oxcart a wheel dropped into a rut deeper than the others and a tire burst. The truck began swinging wildly as the driver sawed at the wheel. If we'd been going down hill we would have overturned, but with a last wrenching of the wheel and a slow easing on of the brakes we scraped to a stop on the edge of stones that marked the shoulder of the road. We cautiously unwrapped ourselves from each other and climbed out so that the driver and his helpers could change the tire. No one protested or said anything to the old woman. Traveling wasn't any easier for her than it was for us and we helped her down, her jaws working even more excitedly on a new nut.

The hillside where we'd stopped was almost barren. Nothing green was growing. The vegetation, even the thin covering of spiny bushes, had been stripped away by the hungry cattle moving desultorily through the countryside in village herds. The only bits of dusty leaf left were on plants that the cattle didn't eat. There were a few shapes of trees, hazy and wavering in the heat, a few hundred yards from us. We straightened cramped legs with the stiff movements of insects crawling from an old skin, slapped hopelessly at dust on shirts and pants. Most of the men were in robes and as they lifted their arms to shake off the dust they looked like short-winged birds craning their shoulders. It was too far to get to the trees through the heat. I gingerly picked a path through the dessicated fingers of the thorns and crouched under one of the plants which had a few leaves left. They were dust-covered and shriveled, but they were leaves and they cast an irregular patch of shade, its pattern falling on the stones like a child's cut-out. Only my head and part of a shoulder were shielded from the sun, but it helped a little as the sun beat soundlessly on the bushes, trying to get at me. Each straggling bush by this time had someone crouched under it. Only two or three of the women were still moving, their robes like almost disembodied shadows as the women moved aimlessly over the hillside, digging up small, twisted roots that they dropped into their clenched bundles.

I sat for an hour under my skimpy bush dreaming of wet handkerchiefs to cover my head, of pans of water to splash over my shirt – all the while watching the driver and his helpers struggle with the sagging gray snake skin of the tire. Finally they straightened up, wiped the perspiration off their faces with grimy sleeves, and flopped the truck down again on the rutted surface of the road. With stiffly stretching legs and the wavings of flapping sleeves we climbed up from our spindly shelters and gathered again around the sagging canvas curtain at the truck's back.

It was late in the afternoon when the truck finally came to a stop, settling in its hanging shroud of dust. Through an opening in the canvas side I could see the river's slick green surface. The place I was looking for was on an island in the middle of the channel and the truck had pulled up at the ferry landing. Most of the people from the truck clambered out and went unsteadily down to the water, kneeling on the dirt bank and plunging arms and faces into the stream. Their skin lost its dull redness and glistened again with its shining black. Telling myself again what sicknesses I could get from the water I sat on the ground and tried not to feel the caked dust lying in sweaty layers on my skin.

On the bank of the river beside us was a small roadside market of food and supplies spread out on leaves under the shade of the thick trees. People were squatting in the shadows, waiting for the ferry or looking down the road for an approaching truck to take them further.

Handmade tables were set up, a few chairs made out of boxes. It was noisy and confused, and only a few donkeys, biting through dried mango pits with machine-like jaws, hairy brown sides heaving with the heat, seemed aloof from the tumult.

The ferry was a dilapidated wooden platform that floated between two sagging wire cables. We lined up on one side of it and pulled on a cable, the man behind me warning me to watch for broken strands of wire: 'They tear your hand.' It took us five minutes to pull ourselves across, like a determined group of ants struggling with the body of a wasp, the sluggish platform of oily boards following reluctantly after us. The place, Georgetown, that I was looking for was a mile further. A truck coming in from an agriculture station was on the ferry, and the driver lifted the canvas sides to let us climb in.

I could see out through the sides as the truck came into the village. Dirt pathways between uneven walls of woven reeds, yellow grass peaks of hut roofs through the stringy leaves of bristling trees, garbage heaped at turnings of the path, goat droppings strewn on the trodden dirt. Crusted troughs of sewers, noises of a distant market, forlorn bellowing of cattle tied in the dessicated spaces of the compounds, blinding gold of grasses tied to the sides of the houses, peeled sticks lashed to gates, dried bunches of leaves fallen against burning metal roofs.

The Victorians, with their unblinking persistence, had again preceded me. The island's name was MacCarthy, or 'Macarty' as it comes out in Banjul, and Sir Francis Burton mentioned it in 1863.

> ... This butt-end of the habitable world, a swamp six miles by four, derives its name from the late Sir Charles MacCarthy, whilome governor of Sierra Leone, who in 1823, by the mistake of his ordnance-keeper in bringing up biscuits and macaroni instead of ammunition, was beheaded by the Ashantis at the battle of Assamacow, and whose name is still sworn by on the Gold Coast. The island in question is situated some 180-200 miles up the Gambia – our charts give a direct distance of 110 and an indirect of 170 – a river so tedious and sluggish that the tide can be felt for 170 of its 300 miles. It is, however, the key of the interior, and a depot of trade, without which Bathurst would soon see an empty market. Consequently we maintain there, in the most tattered of forts, two officers, two assistant-surgeons, and forty-one men. In 1837 and 1839, bilious remittant deepened to yellow fever at Bathurst and

MacCarthy's Island; in 1860, the medicoes died off in rapidest succession, and the non-professionals, out of decency, followed suit ...*

Captain Hewett, who got to the island on the supply boat from Bathurst, was less rigorous.

> ... A few hours more steaming and the island of MacCarthy is reached, which, being the most insalubrious spot in the most pestilential climate in the world, and situated almost on the confines of the limit of the known world, excited astonishment in the beholder, who, surprised, views extensive cultivation, marvels at seeing broad regular streets, substantial well-finished stone houses, and good roads. It is inhabited by two officers (the seniour of whom is governor, magistrate, and barrack-master); a surgeon, merchants' agents, or clerks, coloured people; Acoos, Mandingoes, Jolloffs; and is frequented occasionally by certain wandering tribes ... During the rainy season the island is almost flooded, but as it abounds with game, the love of sport, together with the high pay, induces officers to accept the command, although young men who in the rainy season have gone there with black hair, have returned in three months confirmed invalids, with gray locks!**

As I climbed down from the truck I could see that the village, bunched on the north side of the island, had once fitted both descriptions. I could see that at one time it had been carefully laid out, streets planned, and some permanent building erected, and I could see, also, that at some point all of this activity had faltered, and finally had come to a stop. One street was lined with shambling wooden buildings, most of them poor shops, and I made my way along it, feeling the heat pressing down on my head and shoulders with its dead weight. I was too stiff and caked with dirt to care what the village might have been like once – I had to get the dust off me. I found the government resthouse in an overgrown garden behind the old commissioner's quarters, dropped my bag in a corner of one of the empty rooms and pulled my clothes off a little at a time, shaking the dust that covered them into an old drain set into the floor.

When I woke up the next morning I was thirsty and I walked along the main street looking for something to drink before setting out to find the 'slave house'. An incongrously new sign for 'Fanta Cola' was

---

* Sir Richard Francis Burton, *Wanderings in West Africa* by A.F.G.S. (London: Tinsley Brothers, 1863), p. 166.
** Hewett, *European Settlements*, p. 274.

hanging on a green painted building on a corner. Inside, it was darkly shadowed – the usual shelves stacked with bolts of cloth, cheap cooking pans, cans of meat and fruit, lanterns, and plastic sandals. I could see the usual handful of loafers, the usual fat, swarthy trader behind the counter. His wife, looking worried and even fatter, was sitting on a raised platform behind him with heaped papers and small scatterings of merchandise in front of her – a much handled box for money. A daughter, still slim, but drably anticipating her fate, stood beside her in the red and purple folds of the shop's best dress.

The trader brusquely ordered the men at the counter to move out of the way, visibly struggled with his disappointment when I asked only for something to drink; then sent a boy working for him to get a bottle out of the ice box. I drank it down without looking at it. It was so sweet and thick it seemed to coat the inside of my mouth, but it would have to do. The trader spoke a little English and he began talking, asking me what I was doing there, and how I'd come. Did he know of the old slave building? Some confusions. He asked the men who'd been standing near the counter. They talked among themselves. What building did I mean? The old 'slave house'. He thought about it for a moment, and then nodded.

'That building you mean, I bought it.' He talked rapidly in Mandingo to a man standing near the door. 'He take you.'

I picked up my dusty bag, ready to follow the man, but outside another man stopped us, hurrying out of the building. He was drunk, but in good clothes, hair graying, his face lined.

'That man,' he pointed to the man who was supposed to lead me, 'he doesn't know. He's not from here. I take you. I'm the chief's nephew.'

The other man looked upset. I shrugged, gave him some money and he slipped around the building as if he wanted to get away from both of us.

'I take you,' the chief's nephew persisted, wiping his hands on his checkered trousers, 'but first you buy me spirit.'

I said I'd find him a bottle of beer, but I wanted to go alone. All he had to do was show me the direction where the building was. I was surprised at the obvious confusion over which building I was looking for, but there seemed to be so little to the settlement I didn't think it would be difficult to find anything. As we walked along I could see the old commissioner's building through the trees. The vast screened porches were stained and dark behind the untrimmed bushes. The stucco had discolored and the paint was peeling off the window frames. A square walled prison loomed across the road from the commissioner's residence. We went on, passing behind the painted buildings of the school, with sounds of children's voices hanging in the air like softly colored paper streamers. He led me to the dark opening of another store, the store keeper watching us dubiously as we entered. He clearly had had troubles with the grizzled old drunk before. A surprised look when I told him that I'd buy the man a beer; then a shrug, an apology that he had only a few bottles of imported beer. It was a Moslem village, and because of this there was a religious prohibition against alcohol. The man with me took a few steps back toward the door with his bottle of beer, then shook his head in discouragement. It was too far for him to go; since he was an old man, but I could find it for myself. It was east of the village, the place I was looking for.

'Jang Jang Bure?'

He nodded emphatically. 'Jang Jang Bure. I been here all my life. Not like the other man. On the road.' He gestured vaguely. 'Away from the village.'

When I was rid of him finally I stood looking around me. I could see a dirt track leading into the bushes, and I began walking along it. Outside the buildings that marked the edge of the village there was no shade. Ahead of me I could see wandering cattle, their ribbed sides the color of the dirt, pulling at the withered leaves with hungry mouths. The burnt earth was so thick with their hardened droppings that in the clear spaces it looked like a field of stones.

I was following a twisted dirt track that pushed its way through the dun screen of vegetation. A truck had driven over it, but I couldn't tell, in the soft dust, when it had passed. I couldn't tell if I was coming toward anything. The only landmarks I had to follow were hazy trees, and they slid out of sight behind the tangled branches as I got close to them. After an hour I had to stop. It was too hot to go on, and the track had divided two or three times, and I didn't know if I was on the right one, or if there was anything on the other end of this meandering trail through the brush. I had to get out of the sun and I crouched under a fallen tree, listening, looking around me. So few sounds. I had thought it would be noisier. A few distant birds, a buzzing from some flies, the wind shaking itself with dry gestures as it moved slowly through the rattling branches.

I still felt compelled to go on, and I waited until I could face the sun again and crawled out into the open. My head was beginning to ache, and I felt the glare in my eyes like a sound that continually got louder. Then the trail divided again and I found a truck parked under a tree, a patch of green field beyond it. I could see a dozen figures working in the distance. I'd come to an agricultural project. I went closer. 'Jang Jang Bure?' I called across the distance to them. Figures straightening with the beginning of the day's stiffness, black hands shading eyes against the glare to see who I was. The name didn't mean anything to them, and they didn't speak English. One by one they bent over their rows again, leaving me standing at the edge of the field.

I looked around helplessly. The track seemed to end where the truck was parked. But I could see another turning, a faint trail going off toward some distant trees. Was it there? Probably there was nothing there except heat and thorns. I felt a little like the early European travelers must have felt as they plodded on for month after month looking for cities that were 'two days walk', a 'five days journey', for villages that were 'only over the ridge'. The sun had dropped now until its face was only a surly, darkening ball hanging just out of reach of the trees, but the air was still hot, the wind a dry breath in my face. I walked slowly back, squatting again when I felt myself losing direction. I felt the same sense of relief the early travelers must have felt when I passed a man with a long switch driving in a herd of cattle, and as I skirted the ruins of an abandoned hut I came in sight of the grass huts at the edge of the village.

A buzzing darkness, and I lay on a bed in the resthouse under the shaking blades of an overhead fan that trembled in its slow whirling over my head. I was stripped, still drying from a bath in sun warmed, dirt red water, one of the faded bed spreads wrapped around me as a robe. I had tried to make some notes, with a traveler's sad determination, but the paper was lying on the floor, half lifting as the fan swirled over it, the pen forgotten beside it, as if I'd started some kind of game and then given it up. Just as the sun was setting, a police constable, busily repairing his car beside his house, had finally sent me to what he thought was the 'slave house'. It was a stone ruin close to the river, the roof gone, the doorways only crumbling openings in the stone. The floor inside had been broken into pieces and pushed aside by the weeds and grass. It could have been an abandoned church, except for the blind surfaces of the walls, unbroken by windows. I could see, from the pathway worn through the grass, that people used the building as a short cut to the river bank. Twice, as I leaned against the wall, looking up over the weathered stones into the darkening sky that gaped above them, young men slipped inside the door openings, knelt, and urinated. I had found 'Jang Jang Bure,' but there was nothing to find.

The fan above me went on with its buzzing. I tried to write again, picking the paper off a damp spot on the floor where the gusts from the fan had blown it. I didn't have much to write – only that the consciousness of slavery which dominated so much thought in countries like the United States was so vague here that when I spoke about a 'slave house' no one even knew what building I was talking about. I was also sure that the griot didn't know either; since the building – even in ruins – didn't look old enough to have been built during the period when slaves were being bought. Also it had been built by Europeans, and slave trading along the river had been completely in the hands of the Arabs and the local chieftains. What I'd come across was probably the old warehouse for the trading station.

Three or four men had come into the rest house. They were sitting around a table talking in the large room at the end of the corridor. I dug down into the bottom of my bag for a can of fruit and pried it open with a rusty opener. I wrapped the bedspread around my shoulders and sat in the doorway looking out at the string of lights swaying through the trees toward the center of the village, trying not to think of the dust hanging in its sepia clouds, waiting for me on the road back to Banjul.

5

Toolongjong

The narrative that Alhaji Fabala had sung for me – when I was able to go through it from my tapes and do a rough translation with Musa Camara a few days later – was simple and direct. It was not what would have been defined as 'historical' in a European sense. Much of it was concerned with the names of the people who had been involved, with the kings and their lieutenants. Certainly if someone were presenting this as an entertainment it would be the names that would be most important. In West Africa, where families links are held in such esteem, and where a name is an identification of place and status, the family name would be the thread that held the listener's interest. There were no dates. There had been no system for keeping records; so the European obsession for knowing exactly when something took place wasn't a concern. He had no dates for anything else in his historical narratives; they only related to each other in a kind of resilient, sinewy web.

I realized that it would have been possible with some research into European sources to clarify dates and names, but what he had presented was a different history. The only word I could think of for it was symbolic. It was a history told in symbols rather than in specific details. When he intoned the numbers of slaves and animals that had been presented to the king the numbers symbolized the act of presentation – they were hardly a recital of what would be called 'facts' by a European historian. In terms of European historiography his narrative was almost useless – without dates, the places only vaguely identified, the relationship between the king and the vassal tribes not discussed, and so forth – but for me it was remarkably revealing. What I saw in it was the consciousness of a relationship between Africa and the Africans taken to America, and an acceptance of the roles that all of the parties involved had played in those distant events. It was the first description

of what had happened that had sounded 'true' to me, it had happened
to someone, and if the names and the places he included in the narrative
weren't the actual names of the ancient kings who had confronted the
Portuguese they certainly symbolized what had happened at this
meeting and so many other meetings like it, as the two cultural systems
slowly groped for ways to understand each other.

His own title for the narration was 'Toolongjong', but I found
myself thinking of it as a song, because of its divisions into verses and
the sung passages of praising. As the story unfolded in the long sessions
of translation I also felt it was the most important single piece I'd
recorded.

THE SONG OF ALHAJI FABALA KANUTEH

Toolongjong is the song that was sung for Sunyetta the king of Fuda.
This same Toolongjong was also sung for the great soldiers of Sunyetta.
This Toolongjong was sung for Musa Molo, the king of Fuladu,
for Seneke Jammeh, this Toolongjong was sung for Koree Danso,
for the Sang Kala Maran,
this Toolongjong was sung for Mansa Demba of Berending,
this Toolongjong was sung for Wahls Mandiba.

Now I will tell you how slaves came to be sold to the Europeans.
How it came about is what I'm going to tell.
In that time Mensa Demba was the king of Nomi
and Seneke Jammeh was the king at Bakindi Ke.
There were two wharves, one at Jufred Tenda,
and the other at Albreda Tenda,
and anyone who went there, to Youmi Mansa, went to the king there,
that is king Mansa Demba, and to the queen called Kodending.
If they got hold of any slaves they took them to Mansa Demba and sold
them to him.
At this time Han Sunyetta was the ruler of the world.
He made a king for the village of Sillia,
and another king at Salum, and another king at the village of Baul.
Another king Marujang and Gao.
Before that Satifa Jaware and Fakolly Kumba,
and Komfatta Keying and Nana Jibril.
They were the strongest of Sunyetta's soldiers.

Then the Europeans came,
at that time the only Europeans were the Portuguese.

When the Portuguese came they brought their ship to Sani Munko and
they left the ship at Sani Munko and raised their flag there.
Mansa Seneke Jammeh sent people to Sani Muno to see them.
The messengers arrived at Sani Munko and they found the Portuguese
there and the Portuguese asked them questions.
The first man they saw was Kambi Manneh and the Europeans asked
him what was the name of the place and he told them,
'My name is Kambi'
and they wrote that down for the name of the place, Kambi.
And they came to this place and they found people cutting these sticks
called the 'bang' and the Europeans asked them,
'What are you cutting?' and they said they were cutting the sticks
called 'bangjolo', and the Europeans wrote that down for the name.
Then the Europeans said to Seneke Jammeh, 'We are looking for
something,'
and Seneke Jammeh asked them, 'What is it?'
And they told him, 'We are looking for slaves.'
Seneke then went to Tambana and fought with the people of Tambana,
and fought with the village of Baria.
When he had these slaves he went and sold these slaves to the
Europeans.

The leader of the Europeans was called Wampiya,
and he took the slaves to the city of Salamki Joya.
He went with the slaves to the Hollanders,
that is to the people of Holland,
and he sold the slaves to the Hollanders,
then the Hollanders took the slaves to America.

Then Musa Molo, the king of Fuladu, took four slaves and gave them
to the men called Dikori and Dansa.
He told Dikori and Dansa to take the four slaves to the place called
Youmi Mansa, to Seneke Jammeh,
then the two messengers said to Seneke Jammeh,
'We were sent by Musa Molo to bring these four slaves to you and sell
them to you, to sell them to you for gunpowder and white cloth.'
Seneke Jammeh said, 'Well, it's true we sell slaves to the Portuguese,'
then the Portuguese took the slaves to the Hollanders,
and the Hollanders took them to America.

So then they took the four slaves and sold them to the Portuguese and the Portuguese took them on their ship and sold them to the Hollanders and the Hollanders took them to America,
and when they got to America they sold the slaves there.
Then Dansa and Dikori returned to Musa Molo and told him that they sold slaves at Youmi.
And Musa said, 'Is that so?'
Then he said, 'I would have taken my army to the people of Youmi and fought them.'
Then Musa went with his people to Kunti Wata, to Mansa Burekamara.
Mansa Burekamara gave Musa Molo 300 and 3 slaves,
and then Musa Molo left again.
He went to Alman Basise of Yani,
who was together with Bamba Esa Jamili,
and each of them gave Musa Molo 300 and 3 slaves.
Then he went to Lyama Banta, to Ngari Sabally of Kachamb.
Ngari Sabally gave him 1000 slaves.
He then went to Jatta Sela at Toro Koto with those 1000 slaves and when he came to Jatta Sela with those 1000 slaves,
Jatta Sela told him, 'I will give you 400 slaves.'
And then they went to Samkarangmarong and he, too, gave Musa 300 slaves.

Then Musa crossed the river,
He left the Jokardu district, he came to the village of Tambara,
and to the villages of Baria and Darselami,
he sent a message on to the village of Bakindiki,
and the drum was beating there.
The drum was beating at Berenkolong.
Another drum was beating at Berending and at Jinakibarra,
and another drum at Tubabu Kolomb.
The drums were beating to say,
Musa Molo is coming.

When they arrived they sent a message to the queen
Musa Mansa Kodending and to Seneke Jammeh
and another message to Bumyadu
and another message to Berending
and another message to Sangako
and another message to Misseramding

and another message to Missiraba
and another message to Jinakibara
and another message to Jinaki Kajatta,
and they said, 'Musa Molo, king of the east has come
to visit the king of the west, Mensa Demba.'
Then Mansa Demba said, 'I will send a message to Seneke Jammeh,'
and they sent a message to Bakindi Ke.
When the message came to Bakindi Ke the people then got ready and they said,
'Musa, we know what you want,' and they gave him 100 slaves.
100 young girls. 100 women. 100 young boys.
Money, 100. Gold, 100. Cows, 100. Goats, 100. Sheep, 100.
Musa then said, 'If there is to be a war you can see that it is only because you have something we want to have.'
Then he said to the people of Bakindi Ke,
'There is no war between us.'
He said to the people, 'You have divided your land between two villages, Aladabar and Jufering,
and these two villages took slaves and sold them to Sanneh Munkojoyeh. Since you have been doing this,'
Musa said, 'I would like to meet the Hollanders themselves.'
And the people told him that it was the Portuguese who came,
and not the Hollanders themselves.
'But when the Portuguese come we will take you to the place.'
Then they took the Portuguese to a river place,
the place they called Jang Jang Bure,
that is the name of the two brothers there.

Then when Musa Molo came he collected all the people of Fuladu,
from Ndorma up to Santangto Budu Tabanding.
Up to Santangto Wuruma. Up to Chargel.
He collected them all and he said to them,
'Let us build a house at the place of the brothers Burre and Jang to put the slaves in,
and then sell them to the Europeans.
If we build that slave house then we can
sell the slaves to the Portuguese when they come
with their ships to sell them to America.'
Then they built the house, and up to now the house is still there,
the kind of house the Europeans used to call 'Slave House'.
The building is still at Jang Jang Bure.

At that time when they sold the slaves,
the people who caught the slaves for Mansa Musa Molo were Dikori,
Dansa, Malam Balatema, Yungka Mandu, Kemo Sarata, Funjungu
Kemo,
they were the people who caught all the slaves,
and Dembo Danso was also among them.

When the Europeans came,
when they brought their ship from Portugal,
the ship used to start its journey from Banjul,
then it went to Sanemunko Jammeh, and Mansa Demba Sanko,
and Samkala Marong, and Wali Mandeba, and Jata Sela.
Anyone who had slaves they collected them all together and took
them to the places called Aladabara and Jufure to sell them to the
Portuguese.
Then the Portuguese put them in their ship
and left there and went to Jang Jang Bure.
When they arrived there they went
right to the slave house to collect slaves there
and take them to the Hollanders.
Then the Hollanders collected them and sent them to America.
It is because of this
that slaves are plenty in America.

They call them American Negroes.

6

Some Young Griots

In a town as small as Banjul word spreads rapidly if something unusual is happening, and other people began to notice that someone was interested in the griots and the jalis. In the market I began to see people I'd met at the jalis' houses. Two or three days after I'd been to Bakau there was a polite note waiting for me at the hotel, telling me that two young Mandingo jalis would be playing at a small party in one of stucco buildings a few blocks from the river. It was after nine in the evening before I finally found my way to the house. It was quiet in the streets, and except for the gleam of lights at the corner cigaret stands it was still and dark. In some of the compounds there was the yellow glow of a lantern from the inside of a room, but most of the windows along the streets were dark. I could see the curtains swaying softly in the light wind, but they moved without a sound, as if someone were continually slipping away from the window and then coming back to it when they thought I had passed.

As I came close to the building and then stopped below it, I could hear the music from a window on the second storey. The light, silvery sound of a kora blended against the delicate dry tone of a balafon, and I could hear a voice singing softly in Mandingo. I walked slowly up the stairs, trying to feel my way in the darkness, listening to the voices and the sound of the instruments, hearing laughter and a low murmur of conversation in darkened windows beside me as I felt my way along the coarse wall to the door of the room where the music was coming from.

Inside, a half a dozen men were sitting on hard chairs, two or three in undershirts, the others in shirt sleeves. They were wiry, muscular men, used to hard work. There were two young women with them, in European dresses, but without makeup and their hair in traditional lines of plaits. The furniture was simple, some chairs, a bed, a cabinet, all of it of wood with a cheap veneer finish. A bare light-bulb was hanging in the center of the room. The only obvious difference between the scene in the room and a room like it in any other country was that no one was drinking alcohol. They were Moslems, and the bottles on the table were filled with soft drinks or juice. They looked up when I came inside the door, waved a greeting, three or four leaned over to shake hands, and then they went back to their own conversations or to the music.

The two musicians were sitting on the floor, their instruments in front of them. They were in shirts and light trousers, their sandals put aside so they could curl their bare feet under themselves. The balafon player was about twenty, with short hair and a broad, friendly face. The kora player was thinner, and three or four years older, but they were from the same village and they had been playing together since they were boys. Like young musicians everywhere they let the instruments dominate the music. There wasn't the same care with the recitation that I'd heard from older jalis like Alhaji Fabala Kanuteh, but the mallets hurried over the keys of the balafon and the kora player's fingers flashed on the strings when they played the instrumental interludes.

The music had a light, staccato sound. Both of the instruments are delicate in tone, and when a balafon player is accompanying a kora player he handles the mallets very lightly so he won't cover the sound of the other instrument. The men and women in the room were tapping their feet, one man clanking a ring against his bottle. Often kora players have someone to tap the rhythm out on the body of the calabash while they play, so the clanging was as much a part of the tradition as the figures the balafon players used to end the phrases of the song. When the balafon player did a fast descending pattern, then ended it with a rattle up the wooden keys, there was murmuring and nods of appreciation in the room.

I found, however, that without someone like Musa who spoke enough English to tell me about the songs, I didn't know what they were singing. Many of the songs they did were already familiar – the tales of kings and warriors I'd heard from Jali Nyama Suso – but often it was a melody that was unfamiliar, and since they were singing in Mandingo I could only try to understand what the song was about by glancing at the listening dark faces around me. I thought of it then as part of the excitement of the evening, as something that lent a little exoticism to the music, but it was to become a problem when I met the two jalis again.

I'd gotten to know another man who was familiar with the singers, a man in his fifties named Aliu Dabo. Aliu was a thin, graying, quiet man who had been a school teacher in the countryside – or the 'provinces' as he called the area upriver – before he moved into town. He was a Serrehule, but like most Africans he spoke two or three languages in addition to his own Serrehule and English. His English was clear and soft, still retaining many of the speech patterns of the English colonial schools, even though it had been years since he'd been in the classroom. He and his wife had a room in a compound at the edge of Banjul, and most of the other people in the compound with them were related to them in some way or other. Their own room was crowded with two large beds, home made chairs, a table, and a cabinet against one wall. The room was dark, and it was sometimes stuffy from the small pan of live coals that his wife set in the middle of the floor to keep food warm, but it was large enough for me to sit comfortably on the floor with my legs stretched out in front of me.

Aliu was able to tell me a great deal about the griots, but even more important, he was able to give me some of his own sense of the griots and their music. If you work too much with ethnic music as a field of study you forget that it has a completely different reality to people who have grown up with it. They don't hear it as a cultural artifact. They hear it in terms of the person performing it; they hear it as personal and individual. It is so much part of their own memory and cultural habits that they are often much more interested in variety or change than the outsider studying the music, who wants to fix it at some point of time in the society's development. Ironically, the most dishonest thing a field collector does is collect – since he brings back only objects or examples, and to present them by themselves is to strip them of the associations that someone within the culture brings to them.

Whatever the problems are in isolating the musical expression of another culture, the difficulties with art are even more complex.

Artistic masterpieces from other cultures are taken from their settings – the temples or buildings where they were placed – put into a case, and labeled something like 'Cult Object, early 19th Cent'. It's as though someone from another culture were to 'collect' a Raphael Madonna and put it into an ethnic collection as a 'Religious Cult Painting, pre-Industrial period'. In the cataloguing of ethnic art there is no consideration of the individual who created the work, only its classification as an object. A recent field expedition to the Asmat area of New Guinea worked for several weeks gathering statues and carvings from one area, and before they left they spread out what they'd collected in one of their tents. To their surprise the chief of the village came to look at the work, and instead of naming each piece as to its type of object or use he simply identified it by the name of the carver. The individual styles of the artists – which the collectors hadn't even noticed – were so obvious to the chief that he could go through the pieces the way an art critic goes through works in a European gallery, naming who had done each one of them. What was important for him wasn't whether or not the piece was 'typical', but whether or not it was a good example of the artist's work.

Aliu Dabo had this same close involvement with the music of the griots. His own interest was centered in the Mandingo jali and in the kora, but he was almost as interested in the griots of the other tribes. He had begun working with the national radio, reading the evening news in Serrehule, but because of his interest in music he had become a producer for the radio, presenting Jali Nyama every Sunday for a fifteen-minute program. The Gambia is so small and so poor, that Aliu's jobs paid him very little, but he and his wife could get by, and with land he had in his own village up the river he was able to add to the food supply of the compound. The government was trying to collect as much of the griot material as possible for their own archives, despite their meagre resources, and Aliu was one of the men who went into the countryside to make the recordings. His room was always filled with the sound of the kora and singing as his old tape recorder slowly wound its way through tapes he had collected.

'I know from what my great-grandparents have said and what my father has said to me, that griots begin with a man called Swahata,' was

Alhaji Amara Sahone, playing the konting

Jali Nyama Suso

The Fula Jelefos, Baba Jale Sowe, with the calabash, Satala Kurubally, with the one-string fiddle called the riti

a typical way for Aliu to begin an afternoon's talk about griots. Sometimes I met singers at his compound, sometimes I just sat on the floor with my back against one of the beds and listened to him talk. If his wife had food ready she would come in quietly, her robes gathered around her, and put a covered bowl and a spoon on the floor beside me. Usually it was rice and cooked meat, but occasionally it was cooked okra, always with pepper 'to give it some flavor.' Aliu was a devout Moslem, and I sometimes interrupted him when he was praying. He wouldn't look toward me, but I was uncomfortably aware that I had come at the wrong time. I would stand outside his room, in the shadowy gallery that ran the length of the compound building, waiting until he had finished. The talk would begin again where we'd left it. For him the griots and their role were bound up with what he knew of his own history and his religion. And from his description I could understand how the griots had continued to be part of the society, despite the changes they had all lived through. The 'Swahata' he had begun telling me about, when I asked him about the first griots, was a follower of the Prophet Mohammed when Mohammed still lived in Mecca.

'He goes after the prophet,' Aliu went on in his slow voice, 'and wherever the Prophet goes, Swahata would go after him and call out to the people to come and meet the Prophet. So whatever gifts the Prophet got in those days, the best part of the gifts were given to Swahata. And some of the followers of the Prophet were jealous of this, so they grumbled and quarreled about it until one time the Prophet decided to go without Swahata. So as he went about with his followers without Swahata this time they got no gifts at all, because Swahata was not there to shout to the people that the Prophet has come, that he is a great man, that he is a messenger of Allah. Then the followers of the Prophet asked him, "We had a lot of gifts wherever we went in the past, but this time none. Why?" And the Prophet said to them, "This is the reason: the best part of the gifts were given to Swahata. Now you realize that without Swahata we get nothing, and this is why Swahata was given the best part of whatever we had".'

Often when Aliu talked I had the feeling that I was hearing two voices at the same time. What he was telling me was from his African past, with its conceptions of caste and ceremony, but his language often used some of the idioms of an English school book. After his years as a teacher he now had another pupil. Occasionally he looked over at me when he talked, but usually he was stretched out on his bed, smoking a cigarette, looking drowsily up at the curtains.

'This is why in most villages you find the Swahata names very common with the griots. Most of the griots believe that they have come from Swahata. Their profession still is to follow kings or follow the great men known as "marabouts". They follow people who are good, they talk about them, they talk about their ancestors, they talk about their great deeds. They are given money for this. This is how they earn their living, how they earn food for their families, and this is the way it has gone on up to the present day.'

Some people I met still thought of the griots as having magical powers. As an elderly man told me, 'The griots know all about what has happened. All. They don't be like natural men. They don't breathe when they talk. All those names they know! And some of it I think is true!'

Aliu, who knew them better, thought of them as clever. 'They're very clever, these griots. They know a little – sometimes more than a little – about every family name in the village. They can sing and talk about each name, even if they don't know so much. So wherever the griot goes, if he meets someone with the same family name as the name in his village, he begins to sing about this person's family. If you tell him you're a Jabi, straightaway he begins to sing about the Jabis and the greatness of the Jabis. Then you are touched by what he is singing about you, and you give him money. They're very clever.'

Could they tell you much in detail about a family's history?

'Oh no. They have only the persons' names back to the grandfather or perhaps his father, and it is only the names they have gotten from the family and the family of the man's wife and of her relatives. But they can sing about that for a long time if they know all the relatives in the village.'

Could the griots make up verses about anything that happened in a family's life, if someone told them the details?

'Yes, they are very clever in that. If you tell them any story they can make it to be part of the name. They don't need much time to do it. If you give them a day or two days they can have it ready.'

It was perhaps this cleverness that had been part of the reason the griots had been so feared in earlier times, and why when they died their bodies had been left out in the forest to rot.

Other singers came to the compound, but most of the musicians who sang in Aliu's room were Mandingo jali. They sat on a mat on the floor tuning the strings of their koras as they talked with him, pulling their robes out of the way so that the folds of clothing wouldn't interfere with their playing. Sometimes their wives came with them to perform, and once there was a young wife with a small baby, and she nursed the child as she sang. I found that their repertoire of historical songs was small, and that most of them knew the same major pieces. The real interest was in their own interpretation of the story, and in the flow of the singing. But there were also whole new areas of song for me to experience. One afternoon when I came, a 'halamkatt' was waiting for me. The word refers to the instrument of the Wollof griots, the halam, and katt is the word for singer.

The singer, whose name was Alhaji Sait Camara, was a tall, thin man with a shy manner. He wore the brown robes of a marabout, or important man, and he had an expensive gold wrist watch on his arm. The Wollof people live to the north of the Gambia River, most of them in Senegal, and they have a strong tradition of music and singing. They also were among the tribes who were associated with the Europeans, often as translators, and many Wollof words, as well as elements of Wollof culture, found their way to the United States, even though there was never a large number of Wollofs who were sold as slaves.

I was interested in Sait Camara's music, but I was even more excited by his instrument. Again I'd found something that had also become part of the American cultural background. The halam is a small, simply-made 5-string banjo. The shape differs from the banjo, but it's the same instrument, even to the arrangement of the strings and the finger techniques for playing. In the American South, the instrument was adapted to metal frames, and mechanical screws and bolts were used to tighten the strings and the head, but earlier descriptions of it were similar to the instrument the halamkatt held in his hands as he stood talking with Aliu. It was a long curved block of wood about a foot long and three or four inches across. It had been hollowed out like a child's boat, and then a piece of goat skin had been nailed over the opening. A long round stick projected from one end of it; five strings were tied at different lengths along the stick, and they were stretched over a bridge on the skin head. Because it didn't have the newer adaptations of the American instruments there was no way to tighten the head except by warming it, and the strings could only be tied with lengths of skin wrapped around the stick, so the tone was low and rounded. It didn't have the bright jangling sound of the southern banjo. But the arrangement of the strings had the same small drone string tied to the side of the neck for the thumb to play. Strings were tied shorter rather than pulled tighter, since the light instrument couldn't take the tension.

As the musician was talking he was strumming lightly on the strings, and I could see the same ways of playing that were common in the South two or three generations ago. The halam is a difficult instrument to play, but Camara was obviously a master musician, and the small instrument vibrated with its own taut delicacy. He fingered only two middle strings, using the outer strings as drones, but he slid notes on the tone strings, raised tones by pressing a finger on a string he'd just played, and 'pulled' notes by plucking with the fingers pressing the strings. He had long fingernails, but he also used a small finger pick on the first finger of his playing hand. It was made of a piece of bone sewn onto a leather strap. He placed it on the top of the nail and used it on the downstroke, just as the banjo players do today in Kentucky and Virginia.

I was seeing something that had a clear connection with the United States, but this time, ironically, it was something associated now with white musicians in the South. The instrument had been adopted by whites as part of their impersonations of blacks in the minstrel shows, and in the rural areas whites had learned much of the early banjo techniques – the kind of fingering I was listening to in Aliu's room – from their black neighbors. When they were questioned about their repertoire and their style, most of the older white folk banjo players said freely that they'd learned their pieces from a black neighbor or a black musician who'd been traveling through the area. I wasn't hearing the rolling beat that characterized most of this playing, but these regular rhythmic patterns had almost all come in after a certain period of acculturation, since African music is more intricately stressed. I could also hear that there had been influences from kora music on the halam playing. The katt was performing arpeggio passages on his small instrument, passages that were natural and simple for the kora, with its 21 strings played in a double lyre fashion, but were difficult and uncomfortable for his two melody strings pressing against the rounded stick of the halam's neck.

Sait Camara was as shy as his manner had suggested, and his singing was quiet and introspective. The halam is considered an old instrument, and much of the music is from the Mali area, where the slaves had been gathered for the long trek to the coast and the waiting ships. Since he wasn't sure of what I might want to hear, and he wasn't sure of the kind of songs I was interested in, as a skillful griot he simply combined an old praise song from Mali with new words flattering the president of The Gambia. It was a classic griot performance, with a delicate, almost oriental quality to the sound of the halam. He could have been playing a small children's koto, the Japanese instrument, except for the scraping of his finger pick against the head of the halam and the notes played with the halam's distinctive sliding tones. At the same time he was softly singing:

> The days of our President Jawara are good,
> He himself, his ministers, and the honorable members are good rulers.
> President Jawara rules us with kindness,
> Oh, his days are good ...

Aliu Dabo felt that there was still a place in West African society for the griots, although the changes in the way of life would force the griots themselves to change.

'I think it's becoming harder for them, taking it from one angle,' he said decidedly. 'Taking it from another angle, you might find it's becoming easier. That is, if they try to move with the times, try to make themselves modern, learn new things and new ways of playing, new ways of making money – then they may live happier. But if they want to live in the old fashioned way, by going around singing for people and begging from them, I'm afraid there are quite a lot of people who would now say no to the griots. I hear the young men say, "Why should I give money to a griot? He's strong enough to do something, he's healthy. Why doesn't he go work on the farm as I do and not go around begging?" Quite a lot of the children are beginning to say that. I hear it around me. So if the griots want to live in the village in the old way, they will find it difficult in time to come. But those who want to play in new ways, to make shows or make their instrument work for them, they will find it even easier.'

Most of the musicians I was listening to had found a way to live with the new conditions, but some of the less sophisticated griots hadn't found a way to deal with the changes. One afternoon as I walked to Aliu's compound, two young men waiting on a wall hurriedly looked at their watches as I turned the corner of the street and ran ahead of me to the compound's gate. They were in ordinary work clothes and street shoes, but piled against the wall beside the curtain to Aliu's room were instruments. The men were jelefos, griots of the Fula tribe. One man had a large worn calabash, and the other had a one-string fiddle called a riti. The music of the jelefos was not as highly developed as the songs of the jali or the katts, but it had its own rough hardness and personality. Aliu had never met these musicians, but he spoke Fula and he tried to find out how much they expected to be paid and how many songs they wanted to sing. He looked surprised, but as gently as always he turned to me and said in his school English, 'They expect that they will be paid by the minute.' I said that would be all right. Everyone had been paid by the minute since it was also the way the radio archives paid for their recordings and the musicians were used to it.

Aliu said in an even lower voice, 'They are counting the minutes from the time they saw you.' I understood now why they had looked at their watches before hurrying to the gate. I also understood why they had been so pleased when Aliu wanted to talk to them politely about their songs. They listened to him explain that they would only be paid for the minutes they played and sang, and their faces grew troubled. The riti player, a strong looking man in his early twenties, began talking in a loud voice. He started two or three times to go out through the curtain, then came back as Aliu went on talking in his patient voice. Finally the two of them talked between them. The younger one said something to Aliu and then they turned to stare at me, as Aliu translated what they'd said.

'They said they will sing very long songs.'

I replied that it would be all right, and they picked up their instruments to play. The riti was small and simple. A skin head was stretched over the opening of a small dried calabash, and a single string made out of cotton was stretched from a wooden neck – like that of the halam – over a bridge on the skin head to the bottom of the instrument. The curved wooden bow was strung with coarse black horse hair. The musician played a few figures on it, sounding a little like a country fiddler, except that here the Arabic influence was obvious. It was an instrument that had come from the North, over the desert with the Arab trading caravans, and the musical style had come with it. The other man was busy slipping broad silver rings on his fingers; then he lifted the large calabash, its curved bowl-like belly as hard as a board. The way of playing it was again something that I'd seen in the United States. It was the kind of rattling, rubbing technique that was widely used on the novelty instrument, the wash board.

I was a little uncertain when the man with the calabash played his first few notes, but when they both started on a song together I had to shout loudly enough for them to hear me to make them stop. The two jelefos had had no experience with any kind of recording or even with microphones. I'd set up a machine against the bed where I could watch the dials as I sat on the floor, and the microphones weren't too close to the musicians, but it was impossible to make any kind of balance with what they were playing. The riti would play a few notes in its thin, sawing tone; then the other man would come crashing in with the calabash, the silver rings rattling on its hard, hollow belly. It was like trying to hear a whisper as a train passed.

Every time I started the clattering began again, with all the subtlety of someone throwing stones against the metal roof of Aliu's room. He looked thoughtful. The two musicians looked again at their wristwatches. There was more arguing when they understood that they wouldn't be paid for the two or three minutes of thundering confusion they'd played before I managed to stop them. Finally they agreed to try playing without the calabash, and enough music emerged for me to hear the rough simplicity of their style. The riti player repeated a small melodic figure over and over again, humming a drone tone at the same time. The other man sang the sparse chant of the narrative, using a single melodic line that came over and over again. It was like something hewn out of wood, and when they finished they were as winded as if they'd done the hewing with their bare hands. It was a music that hadn't begun to adapt itself to the newer times.

It was not only the style of the griots from the other tribes that had given their music its professionalism, it was also that most of the musicians who had come to play for Aliu were experienced. But one night he sent word to the hotel that the two young jali I had heard 'entertaining' at the small party had come back again to Banjul from their village up the river, and that they would play for me if I were interested. I finished the bread and canned meat I'd been eating and hurried to his compound. They were friendly and relaxed, both of them related to Aliu, and even if I was a stranger, they'd seen me at the party. I didn't know how much of the jali repertoire they had learned, and I couldn't talk to them because of the difficulties with the languages. But with a smile they pulled the instruments into the space between the beds and sat down on the floor beside me, the three of us taking up all the floor's space. As they were going through the difficult process of tuning the hand-made kora to the hand-made balafon, a third young man, also from their village upriver, came in and greeted them. He would sing with them, Aliu told me, looking at them with an almost paternal warmth, even though they were Mandingos and only distantly related to him through his mother's family.

It was when they began to play that the fact I couldn't understand what they were singing finally became a problem. They played some songs I knew, and then they discussed what they wanted to do to finish, playing a little of a melody for me. The melody and its instrumental accompaniment figures were simple and musical, touching in their directness. Aliu leaned toward me to say, 'It is a song called "Tutu Jara," about a woman who wants to have a child, but she can't have a child so she goes out into the forest and asks the snake to help her so that she can have a baby who will be a great king and do great deeds.'

I nodded, and they began to sing. It was a beautiful performance. The three each sang, trading verses, and sometimes singing in unison. After more than fifteen minutes of the music the recording tape was ready to run out, but I felt I had enough of the song. I was completely satisfied with the version they'd done. The next day, after they had gone back to their village, I sat with Aliu and listened to what they had sung, asking him to tell me what the words meant. The first verse was:

> Great men come from great men,
> great men always succeed great men.
> You don't know, fathers are not the same,
> and sons are not the same.
> This is the time that calls for great men.
> > Aliu Dabo!
> Who is descended from the great surname Dabo,
> the husband of a Mambouray woman.

The praising went on and on. It was beautifully, expressively sung, but there was nothing about a woman or a snake or a forest. The last verse they sang before I had asked them to stop was,

> I'm thinking about the great trader now,
> the great trader who is always kind to us.
> A man without shame is always free.
> I have stood in front of great men and they were
> always read to welcome me.
> Who are they? (a shout from another singer)
> They are the people I met in Sefadu and Peyma.
> > This is true! (another shout)

I began to say to Aliu how upset I was with myself for stopping them when Aliu interrupted gently. 'You must remember that these boys are only young griots.'

'What does that mean?'

'They must begin by learning the instrument, the kora and the balafon; then they must learn the melodies. After that comes the praising. They must be able to praise the people they sing before if they want to have any money for what they do.'

'But what about the words to the song?' I protested.

Aliu shrugged and looked down at the floor, his expression apologetic. 'They will perhaps learn the words next year. Then they can sing the song for you.'

7

Drums In The Streets

As I lay in my room in Banjul a few days later I could feel a humid edge to the darkness. The wind was drifting in off the sea, bringing with it some of the water's dampness. I was trying to sleep, but there was a noisy clatter of drums below my window and my head was still aching from the day's heat. I'd let the mosquito net down over the bed and its sweetish smell of dust and insect repellent filled the heavy air. The noise of the drums seeped up through the walls of the room, and from the window there was a dry rattling of palm fronds, the sounds following me across the matted streets as I tried to get away from them.

How often had I read travelers' accounts of African drums in the night! Usually the writers had found an air of mystery about the sound, a breathy romance of Africa and its people, with descriptions like, 'Drums! Drums! Drums! The sound throbbing and pulsing through the steaming night air, filling the darkness with a vision of orgiastic dancing, of dusky bodies twisting in the firelight …' If the travelers had asked someone what the drumming was about they would probably have found that it was to celebrate the planting of the yam crop. I'd stopped to listen to some of the drumming when I was walking back from dinner, and I knew it was boys in the neighborhood practising. Some of them were playing on the traditional carved wooden drums, but most of them were banging on tin cans, old crates, or bent pieces of rusting oil drums. What they were excited about was the next day's celebration for The Gambia's first nine years of independence. The drumming had nothing to do with the romance of Africa or the stirring of elemental passions. It was just boys making noise. I got up and closed the window, pulled a pillow over my head and tried to sleep.

When I woke early in the morning I could still hear drums outside the window. I pushed the mosquito netting away from the bed, stretched, and pulled on my clothes. I wanted to get out into the streets. I'd already seen dusty cars coming in from the countryside with koras and balafons tied in with the luggage, but I wasn't thinking of doing any work. I wanted to use the celebrations to get away from work for a day. Celebrations, however, have their own imperatives, and often they contain elements of the traditional cultures which have disappeared from ordinary life. Perhaps it's their nature as celebrations that puts them outside the cycle of time, and they develop their own traditions which continue when the event or the ceremony causing them has been forgotten. Whatever the reasons, the day was so rich in musical experiences that within an hour I'd gone back to the hotel for the tape recorder and I carried it with me through the streets, recording as I walked through the streets following the crowds.

By the end of the day I had also been reminded again how clear the links still are between West African cultures and the Afro-American cultures of the United States, even if the connections are sometimes drawn so thin they are hard to trace. When I left the hotel and went toward the main square I saw a group of boys half dancing, half trotting along the street. The boys on the outside of the group were beating on a collection of boxes and rattles and metal cans, and a few on wooden drums, just like the group I'd seen practising the night before under my window. As they rushed past they were singing short, chant-like melodies in time with the drum beat. In the center of the group was a grotesquely dressed spirit figure. It was another boy, but he wore a wildly flapping headdress of cloth and painted wood, and his body was covered with a fantastic animal costume. Red stripes were painted over black cloth and ribbons streamed down from all sides of it. People around me said it was a Mokolo dance. The boys were Akus, descendents of the slaves who had been landed in Bathurst by the British naval patrols.

I could hear other groups of boys approaching from the back streets. The rattling of the drums beat on the plaster walls and echoed deafeningly back over the sidewalks. As they surged past me I was forced back against the fronts of the buildings. In one of the groups I could see more than seventy boys dancing around the spirit figure – some carrying hand painted banners, the others with drums and rattles. Could there be so many? Could I have counted some of them twice as they leaped enthusiastically around the spirit figure? He stumbled along in the confusion, his spindly body hung with a felted, festooned costume so heavy it was weighing him down.

The other groups were smaller. I could count twenty, twenty-five boys as they came clamoring past. Hands were raised over heads with sticks that clanged on boxes or tin cans, or other sticks. Tambourines were shaking in the air, the skin heads torn, the metal flanges bent and misshapen. In the center of each group, close to the costumed spirit, was a perspiring drummer carrying the biggest drum, sometimes just a painted wooden box held around his neck with a knotted length of clothesline. On it he pounded out a steady rhythm for the others. The banners lurched along in the center of the jam of figures, the figure in the middle beginning to dance a little shuffle, an orange cape flowing back over the drummers, the trampling bare feet leaving their marks on the dirt of the street.

What was I seeing? Where had I seen it before? It was in New Orleans, on a Mardi Gras morning in the early 1950s. It was the first time I'd seen the 'Indians'. I'd gone out just after dawn, and I'd walked across the city to one of the run-down black neighborhoods off North Claiborne Avenue. Suddenly a group of boys came toward me from a corner. Boys and young men, singing and dancing the old New Orleans street dance steps. Almost all of them were playing something, a battered tambourine, a bell; some were beating on cans with sticks, or beating two sticks together as they shouted little short lined songs, the voices of the ragged chorus answering the lead singer with bits of words and half sentences. In the center of the swaying group, stumbling along in disheveled elegance was an older boy in a wildly colorful costume. It was made of pink satin, with swatches of blue sash, white dyed feathers hanging from the arms and legs, and crowning all of it, a magnificent Indian headdress, its beaded headband slipping down over his painted face.

What I saw in New Orleans was this same procession of a spirit figure, only in New Orleans the spirit had become an 'Indian', through all the confusions of the new culture and the new religion. His costume was an exuberant exaggeration of something that might have been worn for one of Buffalo Bill's Wild West Shows. The songs they were shouting were a jumble of verses from old work-songs and from the city's street vendors, but the choruses often had incomprehensible words or phrases in them. One of the songs they sang went:

> Here we're runnin' in the Indian land,
>> Hey, hey, To Weh Bakaweh,
> We're the greatest in the land,
>> Hey, hey, To Weh Bakaweh,
> No one else can make a stand,
>> Hey, hey, To Weh Bakaweh,
> Red, White and Blue gets the golden band,
>> Hey, hey, To Weh Bakaweh ...

As groups like them surged past me in Banjul, with the same wildly dressed figure dancing in the center, the same lifted hands banging on tambourines and tin cans, the same shouting of voices and bits of melody, I understood for the first time that the phrases I thought were incomprehensible, like 'To Weh Bakaweh ...' must be African, a phrase from one of the languages along this coast, though I was never able to locate it. The boys on the streets of Banjul were descendants of those who did not become slaves, and the boys I'd seen on the streets in New Orleans were also descendants of the same people who, as slaves had made the journey on to the United States and passed on the memory of an African celebration.

As the morning went on the noise grew louder and louder. The entire population of the country seemed to be crammed into Banjul. The mood in the streets was like the shaking of endless strings of bells.

'I march with my school today,' a small voice at my elbow. A little boy had fallen into step beside me, in a starched white shirt and sharply creased blue shorts. He began pumping his arms up and down in an imitation of British regimental marching, pretending to parade beside me as we struggled through the sand close to the market place. 'Will you come watch?'

'I think so,' I answered. Then a woman in a wound turban and a double-folded robe called to him and he turned to hurry back to her. His mother, who smiled at his posturing. He waved again, and I waved back as she led him toward the open gates of the market, a satchel of food hanging open from her arm.

As I made my way close to the square in the heart of the old neighborhood of Banjul, between the market place and the governor's residence, I could see people gathering in the sun. Clusters of school children were standing under the light canopy of trees that edged the square's rusted iron fence, the children as vigorously washed and pressed in their school uniforms as newly opened flowers. The local police force, looking as stiffly ironed as the children in their shorts and light shirts, were straggling into line on the street behind them.

The Independence Day celebrations were scheduled to go on for most of the day, and it was the usual anxious schedule of processions by the school children, a presentation of the Banjul police, games and gymnastics for the children, a presentation of the fire brigade. On one side of the field a row of sagging canvas pavilions had been erected for the government officials to sit through it all. A scalloped canvas fringe hung from the top pole of the pavilions, giving the scene an almost medieval look, except for the glaring sun and the listless droop of the canvas in the windless air. After the school children and the police and the firemen there was to be an exhibition of 'Native Dances by the Peoples of The Gambia'. It was all so British – even though it was a celebration of the country's independence from Britain. The British governors had organized these same kinds of nervous celebrations on this same dull, stone hard stretch of brown grass for more than a hundred years.

For the last two days workers had been trying to bring some life to the drab grass – watering it, trimming it, and then lining it with white chalk lines that involved three or four men standing out in the sun for every three or four feet of line. After much struggling they'd managed to mark the field off into a series of boxes, the lines trailing over patches of brown dirt and patches of equally brown grass. Long, spindly markings made their way bravely toward the fences at the ends of the field. The lines, the square itself, seemed incongruous and dispirited, like a book that had been left out under a tree.

The groups of boys were still surging out of the street openings, but they'd been joined by dozens of other groups, all of them playing drums and clapping and singing as they pushed through the crowds. There were women's groups in their best robes, some of the women playing small hand drums as others sang and clapped. There were blue-robed women from the headwaters of the Gambia River, their ears decorated with shell-shaped gold crescents. A Mandingo 'Jambabongo' group clattered past, men in black crested hats and their shoulders and chests covered with leafy boughs, their drums echoing against the shadowed arcade of the old government building behind the square. Then from behind a group of shabby stucco buildings I could hear the crashing sound of Fula rattles, and I suddenly found myself in an Africa that was a tangle of the present and the distant, half-forgotten past. I slowly pushed my way toward the sound of the rattles and found myself in the middle of a Fula procession.

In the dense press of white robed bodies I could have been present at any moment in the hundreds of years since Europeans first met the Fulas. The dark faces, the tall sharpness of the bodies, the swaying robes, the din of instruments – it resembled a scene from the earliest descriptions. The rattles I'd heard were pieces of dried calabash threaded to a strip of leather and swung in a loop from a curved stick. They were so loud that I'd heard them before I heard anything else. But somewhere in the procession there was every kind of Fula instrument. Men were carrying deep, bowled drums with strips of thin metal nailed to the rims to add to their thudding tone. Behind them were a row of men with xylophones strung from their necks. There were also the one-stringed fiddles, the riti that I had heard the Fula jelefo play.

Close to me were four or five flute players, their hand-carved wooden instruments more than a foot long with a high, sweet tone. I could see five-string harps made from a curved piece of wood – see them, but not hear them, any more than I could hear the one-stringed fiddles in the din. The noise of the rattles was like a hand slapping my face. There were sudden interjections by the last of the Fula instruments, the cowhorns. The Fulas are still herders, and they make stubby trumpets from the horns of their cattle. They play only one note on the horns, bursting in on the thunder around them.

As they played, the procession was slowly making its way toward the square. All of us were pressed together as the street narrowed; the procession moved without much order or direction. We were so tightly jammed that it was impossible to tell what direction we were drifting in. I could hear shouting and whistles blowing at the edge of the crowd, but it was impossible to tell what was happening outside the wall of noise we'd built around us. I found myself in the center of a group of musicians playing on calabashes that were held against their stomachs as they drummed on the hardened backs with metal rings, just as the Fula musician did who'd played for me at Aliu Dabo's. In the crashing rattle of sound that their rings made on the brown-yellow bowls of the calabashes, I lost all sense of where our feet were taking us.

I had a little of the feeling of what it must have been like to be in one of the early wars, when crowds of musicians were in the center of the fighting, like the battle Godfrey Lovar described on the Guinea Coast, not far to the south of the Gambia River, in 1701.

> ... During the Combat the Drums, Trumpets, and other Instruments in their way continually sound; which joined to the cries of the Negroes, make a Noise louder than Thunder. Their Drums are a Piece of Wood, hollowed at one End only, and covered with the Ear of an Elephant, tightly bound over the Mouth. Their sticks are two Pieces of Wood, shaped like a Hammer, covered with Goat's Skin, which give a dull, hoarse Sound.
>
> Their Trumpets are made of Elephant's Teeth, hollowed almost to the End, at the Side of which they bore a small Hole, by which the Trumpeter, who is generally a Boy of twelve or fifteen, blows. These Trumpets give a clear Sound, but without varying the Tone, like Cowherds Horns. To this ... they add an Instrument as remarkable for the Simplicity of its Construction, as it is hard to be described. It is of Iron, shaped like two small concave Fire-Shovels, about a foot long, soldered together, and which form a kind of oval Belly. A Boy holds this instrument by the small end, and with a Stick of half a foot long strikes on it according to the Cadence of the Drums and Trumpets, who are always near the General, while the Fight lasts ...*

The whistles I could hear came from a program-marshall telling us we weren't supposed to come into the square yet. The confusion grew with the noise, and the procession began to fall apart, with groups idling toward the buildings to get out of the sun. Finally we were strung along the edge of the street close to the square, and I pushed through the ring of musicians with their swollen bellies of sun-hardened calabash. Mingling with the crowd pressing against the iron fence lining the square, I could see that the school children's part in the ceremony had gone off well. The procession moved slowly

* *Green's Collection of Voyages* (London, 1745), p. 714.

across the hardened earth and the government officials watching from the canopies erected at the edge of the field were beginning to shift restlessly as the last groups walked stiffly past in their starched blouses and ironed shorts, but it finally finished.

The children's relief when they marched off the field into the shade and the arms of mothers and aunts was so clearly visible that it seemed to stir the fronds of the dusty palms like a soft wind.

Out of the sweating crowd of musicians and dancers pressing in at the gate at the end of the field there emerged a kind of procession that was supposed to make its way into marked areas, each tribal group presenting itself and then waiting to be introduced, performing a dance for the audience of government officials and for the crowd outside. It was at this point – as must have happened so many times before – that the ceremony began to unravel, with the persistence of a loose thread that someone kept pulling. Everybody tried to get through the gate at once. Dancers were seperated from their drummers, the drummers became entangled with each other, the line that was finally formed kept turning back on itself as people tried to get sorted out. Once in place, after a moment's embarrassed silence, the dancers started to perform – all of them at the same time – spreading themselves wildly over the tufts of the wilted grass. I could see the Fula procession I'd been part of struggling across the field, the thunder of their instruments borne along before them, the other dancers swirling around them like dust that they'd stirred up in their passage.

We began clapping our hands along the fence, but the clapping only added to the confusion. It was impossible to tell – through all the noise – which drummers were accompanying which dancers, and the dancers began looking around at each other in obvious bewilderment. Also there was no agreement about how long anything should go on; so nobody wanted to be the first to stop. Lines began to tangle, circles to break apart and wander. Sometime later, when the pandemonium had lessened, it was obvious that the government officials had trickled away. Some time after that the groups finally made their way off the field, a little winded, but still excited, like a horse that's just been raced and hasn't decided yet if it wants to stop running. Drums were still beating under the trees, arms heavy with rattles were still shaking with the rhythms of the dances. A one-stringed fiddle player came through the crowd still playing and people clapped him on the shoulders.

Along the fence we'd finally stopped applauding. There was some laughter, a little self-consciousness.

'We've not tried anything like this before in The Gambia,' a man said next to me. 'It didn't go as well as they hoped, but, still, I think it was a hopeful sign.' He was shaking his head, undecided about whether he should laugh or look serious about it. 'It was very good,' I said, and then added, 'I was very impressed.' He let himself look more pleased about everything. 'Yes, you could say that it was impressive in some ways. I think it does mark a kind of beginning for The Gambia.' Then he smiled, 'When you come next to The Gambia we will have it all organized better.' We began to scatter away from the old square, the sun weighing us down, and we followed the school children to the cooler shadows of rooms and verandahs to eat lunch.

It was still blindingly hot in the streets when I'd eaten but I was too restless to stay inside. There was to be another program of tribal dances at the President's Palace, and as I went toward it I began to see crowds of people and there was a rising swell of music and shouting voices. Outside the Palace there was complete pandemonium as small boys tried to climb the fence to get into the Palace garden, the police tried to frighten them away, drummers made their way in and out of the milling crowd, and groups of women in their finest robes pressed back under the shadows of the trees.

I could hear clattering rattles again from a noisy crowd ringing the fence and the sound of flutes struggling to be heard over the din. It was a group of Fula musicians and dancers. I could see their faces, parts of their bodies through the densely packed crowd. There were two flute players, a man playing a one-string fiddle, and four men rattling on dried calabashes with metal finger rings – just as black musicians on the streets of the American South had drummed on washboards with thimbles or strips of metal wrapped over their knuckles. The musicians wore a mixture of styles, one of the flute players in a Harlem soft felt hat and dark glasses, his flute taped in bright yellow and red stripes.

The crowd's attention was focused on two dancers, hard, strong half-bearded men stripped to the waist and wearing dirty, loose linen trousers. They leaped into the air, they ran at the crowd, they threw themselves into violent spins then hit themselves on the head with calabashes, trying to get a little money out of the people clustered around them. One of them chased some shrieking women, scraping his calabash on the pavement so that it roared like an angry animal. I couldn't get close enough to see them so I held a Dalasi, the Gambia's dollar bill, up over my head. In an instant the dancers had swept an opening through the crowd and pulled me into the center. Close to them the music was deafeningly loud, the flute players doing a shuffling dance step of their own as they played little melodic figures over and over.

A dancer took the money and gave it to one of the musicians; then he grinned, sweating and dusty – and flung himself down on the dirt. He landed on one hand and began wildly spinning from hand to hand – legs flying in a waving circle. He spun around with such speed that it was almost impossible to follow his movements – his trousers flapping like a streamer after him. Then he did a backward somersault onto his feet, hit himself on the head with a calabash that he'd somehow picked up in time with the music, rolled his eyes, and shook out the back of his loose trousers, held his nose, and pretended that all the excitement had made him defecate in his pants.

With a shout of laughter people pushed past me to get closer, and the flute players picked up their little dance step again. The dancer was on his back, his feet behind his neck, and the other dancer was placing coins over the dirty swath of cloth covering his anus, offering them to anyone who would come take them off. He tried to pull women into the circle and their screams of protest dimmed even the clamor of the instruments.

However, drenched as I was in the Africa of the present as I stood in the crowd around the Fula group I still could feel shadows – intimations – of other things that were also part of the American past. When I left the dancers I followed a procession back into one of Banjul's older neighborhoods, and at a corner I found a group in a broad circle around a drummer. It was a mixed group of men and women, all of them with a pair of short sticks that they beat together in time with the drums. The sound, from a distance, was like a sharp, staccato handclap. The men were in their everyday clothes, except for four or five 'officials' who were dressed in a ragged parody of British army dress uniforms, complete with worn sashes, 'medals' made out of silver paper, and police whistles dangling from frayed lanyards.

As I came closer there was a sudden break in the rhythm and the clattering of the sticks doubled in tempo. The tempo had changed because one of the women had stepped into the center of the ring and started dancing, lifting her knees to her chin as she bent her back in a strained arc, her blue dyed robe swirling around her. In a moment she ran out of breath from her strenuous performance, and the beat of the sticks returned to its slower rhythm. Then a man jumped in, the sticks clattered again, and he began dancing and strutting with grotesquely comic movements as two of the 'officials' helped him by holding up his elbows. In a flurry of dust he, too, ran out of breath and the officials led him back to the ring blowing on their whistles as the crowd shouted congratulations.

It was the kind of dancing I'd found described in dozens of accounts of travels on the southern plantations, when the slaves gathered in a ring and clapped hands as one played a fiddle. Just as in the dancing I was watching, individuals had taken turns jumping into the center of the ring and performing complicated steps for the others. The plantation dance was called the Juba dance. A man next to me who was laughing at the dancers grinned and said this was 'the Jola dance'. The dancers were Jolas, the people who had been living close to the mouth of the river when the Europeans first visited the coast. Other people were also dancing with them – some of the Aku boys and two younger men I knew were Mandingos. It was a simple dance that anyone could take part in, and something like this 'Jola' dance could have become the 'Juba' dance because it was simple and without complexities. It was a dance that any slave could join in, whatever his tribal religion had been. Other dances were more closely tied to ritual and ceremony. Not many Jolas had come to the Americas, since few people along the coast were taken, but this dance, or one like it, had made the journey. In the dance's noisy excitement – the dancers became more wildly inventive as they got dustier and sweatier – I could feel again, as I had with the processions of the Aku boys, the long strands that still bound Africa and America together.

The darkness began to drift into Banjul's streets and I made my way back toward the river to find something to eat.

'Did you see me? I was very good.'

Banjul is a small town, and it was the boy again, that I'd seen in the morning. He was out of his school uniform, and had changed to a pair of faded shorts and a tee shirt, but he stood across the street from me pretending to march again, his arms pumping up and down, his small bare feet making a soft depression in the dust under him.

'I saw you,' I called to him, and began pumping my arms and marching in my own procession alone to the circle of light at the corner. We waved to each other, and I went into the darkness again.

At the next corner I heard a dispirited rattling, and the remnants of one of the Aku groups made its way toward me. There were three or four boys playing on rattles and sticks, the costumed spirit figure shuffling slowly after them, his streamers dragging in the dust behind him, and the sweat stained rings of gaudy cloth hanging around his neck. I stood in the shadows and let them pass, remembering a night procession I'd seen years before at Mardi Gras in New Orleans. The last figure in the crowd then, following the floats was one of the 'Indians', his feathered headdress in shreds down his back, his sequinned shirt sweaty and in shambles, his head hanging, only his feet still moving to a lurching dance that he alone was able to hear. If the two of them had seen each other stumbling along at the end of a long, tired day, the African in his shredded costume, the American of African descent in his, they would have nodded to each other in a weary gesture of recognition.

8

A Meeting With Slavery

As the days passed the flat, streaked, sluggish skin of the river stretched below the stucco balcony of my room became a kind of presence for me. I found myself more and more involved in the river and in the circumstances that had brought it into the periphery of history. It wasn't an especially lively presence – on most days its gaping mouth sagged open in a yawn so wide that I couldn't see across it through the dull haze that hung like a stale breath above it. Its only signs of life were the battered boats that went back and forth from the ferry landing below me to the landing at Bara, on the north bank. But I still was drawn to it – to its history – and this, I found involved me more and more with slavery; since it was as a slave area that it had been most important to Europeans. I was also continually hearing about slavery in the songs I was collecting. The griots told me over and over again about slaves taken in war or demanded in tribute by the African kings that their songs celebrated.

As I talked with the griots and with the people I met in Banjul, I asked them more and more persistently about slavery. My questioning finally became too insistent for a man who worked in one of the government offices and who had helped me with the forms I needed for travel into Senegal. His name was Amara Sahe, and he was a Serrehule, like Aliu Dabo. I had gone to his room, a bare, plastered space in a noisy building that was relatively new, but had become even more marked with the debris of children and animals. It had been designed without a yard space, which meant that there was no place to put the usual garbage heap and the garbage instead was scattered everywhere throughout the building. He listened to me for several moments then gestured impatiently.

'You always ask me about slavery.'

'Yes,' I said.

'Then why don't you come to my village and see the slaves.'

I stared at him, too surprised to answer.

'Yes. We have had slaves there from the beginning. Serrehules are great traders and we bought them from the warriors at the time of the wars.'

'You still have them?'

'The slaves now are the children of the slaves from those times, and their children's children, but we still have them.'

I had heard that there was still some slavery in the interior, but I hadn't expected to meet it here in Banjul, in fact, I hadn't expected to encounter it in any way. I didn't know what to say. He shrugged, half smiling at my bewilderment; he had been with non-Africans enough to understand some of what I was feeling.

'I must go to the provinces,' as he called any part of the country outside of Banjul, 'to see my family. If you would like you can go with me.'

I was – again – straying from the prime reasons for my trip, but this was also implicit in the reasons why I'd come, and there was no way I could say no to his suggestion. I was immediately and intensely curious.

Every trip I made away from the coastal areas seemed to be different from any of the other trips I'd taken. Amara's village was about two hundred miles inland, close to the Senegal border, and across the Gambia River on its north bank. It wasn't possible to get to the village in the passenger trucks. He usually went home by taking a truck as close as he could come and then walking the rest of the way. He said there was a road we could take, and I found it was possible to rent a small car in Banjul. The owner of the car asked me closely where I was going, and I assured him, after a moment of hesitation, that I wouldn't be leaving the Banjul area. With a last fond look at the car's worn tires and drab fenders he handed over the keys and watched uneasily from the side of the street as I drove off. When I reached Amara's building I was surprised to find two younger men with bundles and suitcases waiting with him.

'These are my brothers,' he explained, 'and they also are going to the provinces. One is coming to my village, one is coming back to be with his wife. I told them you might let them ride with us.'

He waited expectantly for me to say something. He had put on his best shirt and was wearing a new straw hat. His two brothers were obviously poorer, their bundles small and tattered, their clothing a combination of native and European dress. They didn't understand

English. I realized that his simple request was a common aspect of the West African system of extended familial ties. I was paying him for the days we would be traveling, but at the same time I was making it possible for him to get to his village. He, in turn, felt responsible for his brothers, who also wanted to get to their own villages. Europeans who are unused to this system often find themselves in exasperating situations where a man they've hired brings along other family members with the expectation that they will also be hired – or, as I had found – that a ride for one meant a ride for several. I thought of it simply as another way of defining interrelationships, and as the trip to the village went on there were to be many other moments when I was expected to accept other possible definitions of attitudes and customs. I smiled, motioned to the car, and in a moment the two brothers had squeezed into the cramped back seat, their bundles pushed down on top of the recording equipment.

For the first hundred miles we followed the same paved road I'd taken with the truck on my first trip into the countryside. I was conscious of how much the landscape had changed, even though the villages and the heat of the day seemed to have changed very little. It was now the end of the rainy season, and there was a heavy greenness to the landscape that I wouldn't have believed possible after the days I'd spent walking over the hard, baked earth at the end of the dry season. The cattle in the interior weren't as thin and they had a slow indolence to their gait as they moved from one clump of grass to another. For us in the car, the most decisive difference was that when I turned off onto the dirt road where I'd become coated with dust before, this time the surface of the road was caked and still damp, and it seemed to be gently breathing as it stretched out ahead of us through the brush and trees. There was only a light suggestion of the choking clouds that would come later in the season.

The night before I'd looked at a map of the area where we were to be traveling and I'd noticed that we would pass, on the other side of the river, the site of the small trading station where the first European traveler into the interior, Mungo Park, had stayed while he learned Mandingo and familiarized himself with the countryside on his first journey. A road was marked on the north side of the river, going from a ferry landing west of the site and then continuing on toward Amara's village. When I suggested we might stop to see the site he nodded; even though he'd never heard of Park.

'It should not be difficult.'

I was making two mistakes, though I didn't realize it at the time. A map of the countryside in the United States or Europe doesn't indicate that there is a road unless there is recognizeably something that a vehicle can travel over. The other mistake was misunderstanding Amara's response. He knew as little about the road as I did, but to agree to try to find the place was a subtle way to exchange favors for my giving his brothers a ride.

Because of the better condition of the road it wasn't too long before we reached the ferry landing, and despite the late morning heat the operators were still laboriously pulling the ferry's flat barge-like boat back and forth across the river for the few straggling passengers sitting languidly in irregular patches of shade along the banks. It could have been the kind of ferry landing Park had found when he came to the town of Segou on the banks of the Niger River almost two hundred years before, except that this ferry was made of rusting iron, and instead of cowry shells the operators wanted paper money. The car slithered up the splintered wooden landing ramps and we swung across the river's green, sluggish current in the company of some teenage village girls in long wound skirts and flowing turbans who giggled at the two younger brothers and turned away in nervous embarrassment if I looked their way.

On the other side of the river a dirt track led up from the ferry landing into a dense thicket of grass that towered above the car in broad swathes of green. The track was narrow and rutted, but it was wide enough for the car to slip through the wall of grass. Then on the other side of the thicket the road ended. What stretched in front of me was a meandering foot path, occasionally widening out enough for a donkey cart to be drawn along it. I stopped the car and turned to Amara, who was sitting beside me unconcerned in the front seat. Is it possible to drive along this track? I asked him. Oh yes, he assured me. Could he find his way along it to his village. It wouldn't be difficult.

I hesitated. He couldn't drive a car himself so he probably had no idea how difficult the trail really was, and it seemed possible to me that we could follow the path's wanderings for hours. I'd filled up with gas at the last settlement we'd passed through, but it was hard to believe that I could find any more for the car in the area ahead of us. Sensing my indecision Amara looked at me pleasantly.

'It isn't far from here.'

If we had been in anything but a car it probably wouldn't have been too far, but a car was probably the most useless means of transport we could have taken to get there. But at that moment, still excited by the countryside itself, I was willing to be persuaded. I put the car in low gear and we swayed off along the dusty path, one side of the car tilted down into the worn rut of the footpath, the other side bumping clumsily on the grass ridge beside it.

The villages that stretch beside the paved roads in West Africa are somewhat analogous to the towns of the coast. They reflect the newer social patterns and they aren't representative of the older way of life. In the hours we lurched through the bush, searching first for the starting point of Mungo Park's journey and then for Amara's village I found myself in a world that still had some resemblances to the older Africa that no longer exists beside the highways. It wasn't an 'unspoiled' countryside, but the villages were still isolated and the life was still largely dominated by arduous labour in small garden patches.

Each village still maintained its distinct tribal character; since in their isolation there was less of the mingling of tribal groups that was occurring in the cities. The Mandingo villages were solidly built, the large huts hidden behind the woven walls of compound fences. The occasional Serrehule compounds sometimes had buildings of frame construction and stucco finish, with corrugated iron roofs. The Fula villages, in keeping with their more nomadic herding life, were clusters of simple shelters. I couldn't help thinking that they must have looked much the same to Mungo Park as they did to me almost two hundred years later. The huts were loosely clumped together and despite haphazard attempts at gardening the cattle spilled through the open spaces in the forest with the boys and younger men trailing casually after them. The style of dress in the villages also reflected the tribal differences, from the robes of the Mandingo villages to the shoes and European shirts and trousers of the Serrehule compounds. In the Fula villages the car would be surrounded by young women unconcernedly wearing only a wrapped skirt. They laughed and crowded close to the window to talk to the young men in the back seat. In their villages the only sign I could see of any use of western technology was an occasional flashlight stuck up in the branches of a hut roof.

I was hopeful, with each new village, that we had finally come to some place that the men with me recognized, but I was soon aware that they had as little idea of where they were as I did. The paths we were following went from one small cluster of huts to another, and as the paths trailed in and out of each village they branched out into even thinner trickles. We had to slow down in the center of each village and wait by the uneven log platform used for village meetings until someone came to see what we wanted. There would be long conversations in whatever language the village spoke and Amara would gesture in the direction he thought we should take. After long leave-taking prayers I would put the car into first gear and move slowly along the village's donkey cart track until we came again to the threading of the foot paths.

By late afternoon we were so wrenched and worn by the lunging progress of the car that we had stopped speaking. For a long stretch we wound through an area of low hills, the path scrambling in and out of the stony hollows, leaving us to thread after it through the crumbling redbrown stream of stones that were strewn along its sides. On a twisting downhill path I had to send one of the younger brothers out ahead of me since I could see only a few feet through the choking growth of spiny trees and underbrush. I had given up any thought of turning back, since it would only mean driving back over the same stretch. I wasn't even sure I could turn the car around. As I hung on to the jerking steering wheel I tried not to think of what would happen if the car *did* break down. The anxious owner in Banjul would have to send donkeys out to drag it back to the river and then pull it across on the ferry so that a mechanic could look at it. My only purpose had become the grim struggle to get the car as far as I could take it.

At some points our aimless veerings and the river's equally aimless twistings brought us close to each other and I would suddenly come upon low fields planted with rice. Women from villages hidden in the trees were scattered through the massed green plants, bent and half hidden in the raw growth. Like the women I'd seen under the trees in Bakau village they looked almost bird-like; from a distance like wading birds, their colors some kind of mating plumage. Finally we emerged from the undergrowth only a hundred yards from a short stretch of road and three or four stucco buildings, beside them a blackened pier built on palm trees driven into the mud of the river bottom and planked over. The turgid green of the river's surface drifted in swirling eddies below us.

'We have come to Karantaba. The marker where the man Park stayed is not so far from here,' Amara said tiredly. He was as covered with dust as I was and he wiped his face with a handkerchief that had become soaked and brown from perspiration and dust. After a few moments a boy came out of the buildings beside the river, and Amara called out to him. The marker on the site where Park had stayed was at a place called Pisania, further upstream. The boy would lead us to it if I paid him something. The brothers in the back seat squeezed together so he could sit beside them. A half mile out of Karantaba the track I'd been following ended. The boy began saying something and waving me on insistently. I realized that what he was saying was 'Can go'. Again it seemed as reasonable to go forward as it did to turn back; so I began driving along the edge of a small field, then following his pointing finger I turned and the car wobbled over the field itself, clambering over the uneven ridges left by the hand digging tools. We came to a stop under a tree with a platform built in its lower branches.

As we got out I could see that the platform had a bundle of clothes and a thin loaf of bread thrown up on it. Village boys slept on it to guard the crops from monkeys. Standing stiffly beside the car, shaking out arms and legs to loosen cramped muscles I noticed that it was almost sunset. Soon it would be dark, and if we continued to travel the way we had been I'd have to drive the last few hours with only the car's headlights to pick out the path. I shook off the thought uncomfortably and followed the boy into the undergrowth. Amara, curious himself to see what I was looking for, followed us.

The only thing that was left of Pisania was the depression in the ground where the well had been. A monument had been erected by the colonial government and the space between it and the river bank had been cleared so that the column could be glimpsed from the weekly riverboat, but the bushes had grown in again around the monument. It was in disrepair, and I could see that in a few years it would disappear in the same way that the buildings themselves had disappeared. It wasn't difficult to understand why. Except for a few older school teachers no one I'd met in The Gambia had even heard of Park. The journey he'd taken with such difficulty and written about with such success was an everyday occurrence for African traders of the period. Gambians were as little interested in the story of the first Europeans who'd walked through the countryside as we would be in narratives by the first Gambians to see the Hudson River or Trafalgar Square. The monument was only another inexplicable scrap of the incomprehensible period of colonial rule, and its crumbling would help mark the end of that period.

As we trudged back to the car I was conscious again that this was the only sign I had encountered during the day that there had ever been a European presence on this isolated bank of the river. On maps from the turn of the century the area had been carefully delineated and colored in as part of the British Empire, but the men and women in these villages had gone on living their lives with only a vague and uncertain contact with any central authority. I had a strong feeling that the Europeans had simply exaggerated the importance of their influence on the region – especially since language, family systems, even methods of agriculture and trading had stayed essentially intact. The actual physical presence of the old British Empire on this lonely river bank was a shallow hole under a thorn bush and it would be a kind of cultural egotism to give any more significance to it.

I have only confused impressions of the next few hours. We were still groping our way through a spindly web of foot trails, but we were now doing it in the dark. I have a clear memory of a high bridge of logs over a tributary of the river. It was about fifty meters long, the logs laid in two thin strips over shorter pieces of log tied under them to a swaying frame. It was dusky, in the last moments of the fading twilight. I couldn't let myself hesitate. I knew that if I stopped to get out and look at the bridge I'd be too afraid to try driving over it. The log strands were set too wide apart for the wheels and we began slithering against the uneven underpinnings. The car began to yaw uncomfortably as we closed in on the other side, but when the wheels finally spun off we were across, and we landed on a heaped bank of mud instead of down in the gulf I could see under the bridge.

In the darkness that descended a few moments later we heaved from village to village, stopping at small roadside fires to ask the people sitting around it which way to go. The hillsides became steeper, stonier; then I could vaguely make out cultivated fields on either side of us. We came into a village with stucco houses, there was a glare from a Coleman lantern hanging in a shop. Amara rolled down his window and began shouting to people we passed. We had finally come to the village that lay closest to his compound. We stopped to pick up some food; then after another twenty minutes of driving we came to a leaning corrugated iron fence. There was a dull gleam of lantern light behind it, then the erratic flashing of flashlight beams. The gates of the compound were slowly pushed open and we drove into a small open space against a house wall. I wearily turned off the motor and leaned back in the seat, letting Amara and his brothers greet the members of their family. After a moment I slowly opened the door, slid off the seat and leaned against the car's dusty side, waiting for someone to remember that I was there.

When I tried to write something down in my notebook later my hands were still shaking so badly that when I tried to make it out the next day the writing was almost indecipherable. It was as jagged and irregular as if my body had retained some of its jolting, the way your body accustoms itself to the sea's motion on an ocean trip. I was still shaking as if the motion were now part of me. I was too tired to think, and my mind jerked with the same unsteadiness. I wrote – as closely as I can make it out:

> White plaster walls – closed in a small room – walls crooked and splotched – sagging corrugated iron roof – a water pan in the corner. Trying to see in the light of a candle. A cup upside down on the pan – concrete floor, a low battered wooden chair, a rickety table, a stand for a trunk – (three words impossible to read) – clothes, bowls, shoes, baskets – glass framed pictures with flower painting around family, the bed iron-framed canopied with blue mosquito netting – green cloth thrown over it. Trying to write by yellow light of candle – sounds of men's voices from their platform outside under the stars. Stirrings, a baby whimpering in the women's room next to mine. Murmurings, movements – crickets, crickets, crickets. I have to sleep. It's so dirty I lie stiffly on the bed – sagging with my weight – sound of rats from the corner – candle flickering over rubbed discoloring of the walls – I have to sleep.

From the night I remember the noises around me, the feeling of water on my skin when I took a pan out onto the earth behind the room and spilled it over my body to get some of the dust off me, Amara's tired insistences that I had to keep myself locked in, that all of the doors in the compound were closed shut at night, and I remember the dimly lit bundles of clothing and the low bed frames in the rooms at the end of the building that had been given to what turned out to be the slaves.

I woke at dawn with the movements in the compound. Women and children, chickens, men's voices outside the ramshackle iron fence behind my room. I had slept fitfully. The scampering of the rats, the muffled scratching of their feet on the dirty cement of the floor kept waking me. Amara woke me sometime toward early morning. He had become feverish and needed the tablets that were on the small table across from the bed. He was still weak when he came back with food for me just as the sun rose. There was hot tea and a bowl of boiled millet and milk whey. I tried to shake some of the dust out of my clothes and followed him out into the courtyard.

The compound was much more substantial than most of the dwellings we had passed on our journey. There were two long, one-storey stucco buildings, their iron roofs stretching out over shaded porch areas. The ground was bare and hard, with trampling footprints leveling the packed earth. The men's platform was beside the building where the oldest brother lived. It was a low concrete form, without shade, but set far enough from the building that it caught the night breezes. There were small thatched buildings behind the stucco main buildings, and I could hear the sound of millet being pounded and the metal clattering of cooking dishes from them. The children were playing on the rubbish heaps with the chickens or chasing each other across the courtyard in laughing games of tag.

Amara's father was dead so his older brother was now head of the compound, but his father's eldest wife was still living and she had a room of her own beside the women's quarters. The door of the women's sleeping room was standing open and in the shadowy interior I could see several rough iron bedsteads in irregular rows, with boxes for personal possessions against the wall. Amara led me across the courtyard to the gate of the compound. We dragged it open through the heavy sand and walked outside. There were people from Guinea who had come to work in the fields and they were sleeping in a hut outside the compound gates. The women traveling with them were still inside the building as we passed, their few possessions in bundles on the hut's dirt floor. Their draped skirts were faded and torn, and they were without the usual bracelets or armbands that most of the compound's women adorned themselves with. They watched us without expression as we glanced in the doorway and then went on to the fields.

Scattered through the crudely cleared area around the compound I could see groups of men working. One group was piling sticks along the path, these were the men from the Guinea group. The other men were bent over their short digging tools, working along the shallow furrows. Amara motioned toward them.

'Now you see them.'

'They are the slaves?'

'Yes.'

Some of the men looked up as we walked toward them, nodded at Amara and went on with their work.

'And this is what they do?'

'They have other work when the rainy season comes, but this is their work for now. They are farmers, just as we are traders.'

We went on to the end of the cultivated area and sat on a log. I stared at the men in the field, trying to adjust the reality of their appearance with the preconceptions I had of slavery. The most difficult thing I had to rid myself of was my own cultural conditioning. The slaves were black, but Amara himself was black. They were no different in color from the small cluster of men from Guinea. In every depiction of slavery in the southern United States or South America the color difference between slave and master had been crucial. The slaves were in ragged clothing, but the Guinea men were working in shirts and pants that were almost as torn and patched. Amara's young brothers wore clothes that were only a little better than what the slaves were wearing.

'You see, they have been slaves in my family for all of their lives and this is their work. Their grandfathers and fathers were slaves here and their children will follow after them and be slaves. We did not take them as slaves, because we don't take part in wars, but the warriors sold them to us many years ago. There was a time when there were

*Alhaji Fabala Kanuteh*

The young Mandingo Jalis, from left Dela Kanuteh, with balafon, Aliu S. Dabo, Karunka Suso, with kora, friend, Mawdo Suso, with balafon

The halam, ancestor of the 5-stringed banjo

A Wollof griot, Abdoulie Samba

many wars before the Europeans came and with the wars came many slaves.'

'But don't they try to escape?'

'They have been here all their lives and they wouldn't have a place to go to. Sometimes a man will go away and take himself to Banjul, but people all know who he is so he comes back.'

The men were working steadily along the furrows and I could see no sign that anyone was directing their work.

'Can they become free?'

'They could always be free if they would pay us the money we paid for them. It would not be hard for them, and sometimes they get gifts of money or we allow them to work for another family's compound and they get extra money in that way, but it would take a long time for them to save enough so they don't do it.'

'But they go on doing the work?'

'I know you are thinking that this is all those things you have heard about when you say slavery, but we have all lived together so long that in some ways I think of them almost as my brothers.'

'Could they marry someone from your family?'

He looked down at the ground and then across the fields. 'Oh no. They marry only other slaves. They couldn't marry a woman of our family.'

I asked the last question carefully. 'Could you sell them?'

Amara shrugged. 'You know that it is against the law to sell slaves. It was a law that the British brought with them. They also told us we should let our slaves go, but we had paid much money for our slaves and they didn't tell us how we would be paid if we let them go. So we don't sell them, but it is like we have money in the bank in Banjul. Sometimes you cannot draw it out, but you know it is there all the same.'

'And it is the same with the slaves?'

'Just like that. You see them working and for this we give them food and their room and when they need clothes we give them clothes. But they belong to us, and they will go on living this way until they give us money so they can leave the compound.'

We sat in the shadow watching the men work, but as the sun rose higher they straightened up and went toward the shade of the buildings to get out of the midday heat. Amara didn't know how many slaves there were in the area, but his estimate was that three out of every ten families would be still living as slaves. 'It is only someone like you who thinks so much about it,' he said impatiently when I tried to press him more closely. 'For us it has always been this way, and I don't think it will change for many years to come.'

As I lay stretched out on the men's platform in the darkness after we had finished the evening meal I let myself be suspended in the drifting sounds around me. In the silence of the countryside any sound becomes clear and definite. A battery operated radio was playing inside one of the rooms and the men's voices murmured around me. The two younger brothers were still with us and there was much exchange of news about members of the family in Banjul. I had tried to ask Amara more questions about slavery in the area after we'd eaten, but he wouldn't say anything more about it. He seemed uncomfortable with himself for having told me as much as he had. I found that though some of my questions had been answered I still had many questions to ask him, but I could understand his unwillingness to talk more about it. It is illegal to hold slaves, but his reluctance stemmed as much from his consciousness of our cultural differences, as it did from any worry that I might try to report the presence of the slaves to the local authorities. Whatever he thought about it himself he understood that from my point of view holding slaves was an immoral act.

Lying there on the platform, listening to the voices and feeling the night breeze ruffle my clammy shirt it was difficult to put the whole question of slavery into any kind of perspective. It was obvious that as an American my own consciousness of slavery had been heightened by the Civil Rights struggles of the 1950s and 1960s in the United States. Here, in a small compound isolated in the West African countryside, it was equally obvious that whatever the European role had been in exploiting slavery, the system had been so widespread before the Europeans came to Africa, and it had been so deeply ingrained in African society that vestiges of it still lingered years after they'd left. The man squatting in the dirt close to me, laughing at a story someone was telling, was a slave. The reality of this made some of my own concern seem almost naive. In an effort to clarify it for myself I tried to think of myself only as a member of a different tribe. I told myself my attitudes toward slavery only reflected a different tribal background, not any larger moral concern. But I found I couldn't do it. I couldn't put myself into any position where I could accept slavery. Troubled and quiet, I waited a few moments, then said goodnight and closed myself into the stuffy room.

The same noises of people and chickens woke me early the next morning. Again it had been difficult to sleep with the scratching of the rats but I was still so shaken from the trip that I drifted off with the sound of their teeth scraping on the rim of a metal pan. The sound mingled in the stale air with the whine of the mosquitoes I hadn't been able to kill. The folds of the mosquito net closed everything off around me. Amara came to the room early to tell me that we were to go to the village nearby, the chief was waiting to see me. He was still a little uncomfortable with me after my questioning the night before, but in a moment he had shaken off his embarrassment. After breakfast, again of boiled millet and whey, I put things back in the car and he said his ceremonial goodbyes to his brothers. One younger brother was to ride further with us. We still hadn't come to his village in our wanderings two days earlier. As the people of the compound stood waving to us Amara bent down and wrote in Arabic in the dust. It was a prayer, asking that he be allowed to live long enough to return again. Then he straightened up, put on his hat, and climbed into the car.

The road was good to the village, and we covered the distance in a few moments. Amara had time to tell me that I had asked him once about the flute music of his own people and he had sent word to the Imam, or chief, that I wanted to hear the local musicians. It was, again, a subtle repayment for the service I was doing him by taking his brother on to his own village. He sat back beside me, fanning himself with his hat. He was completely unaware of how often he surprised me.

As I'd traveled through the back country I'd seen many of the trappings of the old colonial period. I'd seen the buildings, the uniformed constables on their bicycles and the old printed notices outside the local offices. In the village I experienced a little of the life of the colonial days. The British District Officers had tried to visit the villages in their districts as often as possible, at first traveling on foot with caravans of bearers, then later on horse back and finally by car. Since the idea of governing was that the local administrators were only supplementing the native chiefs rather than replacing their authority the visits became almost state occasions for the people in the small villages. I got a little of the feeling as we came down the village street, and as I fumbled my way through the morning, trying to think of myself as a British District Officer, Amara had to lean over and whisper to me from time to time what I was supposed to do.

Almost all of the village's people were waiting in the dusty square between the low mud houses, and as we came closer they began to applaud and gather around the still moving car. The Imam, a man in his middle thirties with a small mustache and an elaborate, full robe, was reclining on a bench made of sticks bound to a wooden frame under a hastily erected canopy. He didn't rise when I shook his hand, only nodded politely. We listened to a short talk by Amara, the Imam replied, both of them speaking Serrehule, and everyone applauded again. I was led to a sagging canvas seat at the foot of the Imam's bench and Amara leaned over to tell me that the Imam had wished me welcome. The Imam turned to say something to someone behind him, but it wasn't necessary to send a message. The musicians had seen the car arrive and they were now marching toward us through the trampled earth of the square, their bare feet kicking up a small flurry of dust as they approached.

I was sure that many of the British administrators had had as little idea what was going on around them as I did, but at least they got more practise at it. The musicians stopped in front of me and there was another exchange of speeches and more applause. I was looking at them with considerable interest; since it was a small drum orchestra with a flute player as the main instrument. There were three sizes of drums — all of them handmade, and the flute itself was a crude wooden instrument. I began to set up the recording machine and there was much excitement, and almost before I could turn the machine on the musicians began playing. The flute melody repeated itself over and over, but the drum rhythms were subtly varied, the accents shifting as each of the drum's pattern of beats changed in relationship to the others. When I played back the first piece there were shouts and laughter from the villagers, and even the chief permitted himself a smiling nod of the head.

Again, it wasn't a music that was related to the blues, but it related to the black culture of the southern states. In Mississippi there are little bands still playing flute and drum music. Most of what I'd heard them play had been derived from the fife and drum corps music that had been popular in small towns years ago, but they also played some other pieces that clearly weren't derived from these sources. Music like this that I was hearing in the village was the source for the other pieces – this music, which was Serrehule, and the Fula flute music, both of which had come from this slave area. I had come again to something that tied the African and Afro-American cultures together.

By this time the singers of the village had joined in with the drummers and the flute player, and three elderly women had come from one of the huts in ceremonial dance costumes. The morning had turned into the kind of spontaneous village festival the colonial administrators had described over and over again. I sat in the middle of the singing and dancing, trying to hold a microphone close to the flute player, laughing with the others at the gusts of excitement. By early afternoon everyone was winded, it had gotten blindingly hot, and I had come to the end of the flute player's repertoire. There was again an exchange of speeches. How much should the musicians be paid? I was asked to suggest an amount. Amara whispered in my ear what he thought should be enough for them. The money was taken with considerable dignity and pushed out of sight in folds of robes or shirt pockets. There was another whispered suggestion from Amara. The Imam should also be paid. I presented a small handful of tattered bills; they were accepted with a careful nod. Still without getting up the Imam shook hands again, and with much waving to the villagers Amara and his brother and I gathered up the recording equipment and got into the car.

This time, when Amara said that it wasn't far to the river I shrugged and drove along the foot path he pointed out to me. This part of the country was familiar to him, and we should be able to find our way. I had enough gasoline for another twenty or twenty-five miles. The difficulty, however, was getting to his brother's village. His brother, it seemed, was married to a Fula woman, and she lived in one of the small Fula settlements deep in the forest. By the time we lurched over the same kind of crude trails I'd followed two days before, left Amara's brother with his excited family, and made our way to the ferry landing it was late afternoon. As we clambered wearily and dustily out of the car to wait for the ferry Amara rummaged in his bag and came up with a carefully wrapped pan. He had brought food for us – meat and okra. In another pan was rice. Since I hadn't much experience eating with my fingers he'd brought me a spoon. We sat in the shade of a tree and ate in companionable silence as the ferrymen slowly dragged the empty shell of the boat over the glistening water toward us.

The ruts of the paths we'd been traveling over had begun to have their effect on the car, and as I was afraid would happen, we began to hear a banging noise as we drove slowly in the darkness along the dirt road that would take us eventually back to Banjul. At least we'd gotten across the river, and I could get help in the morning. It sounded at first like something had burned out in the engine, but as we fell into the road's shadowed potholes I realized that it was something in the front axle. We decided to try to get to the next little village – we could possibly find someplace to stay for the night. When we clanked into the dark lines of huts that marked the village we were making so much noise that the people still sitting up – mostly young men gathered around a small bonfire they'd lit close to the village's resting platform – drifted over to see what was the matter. Amara got out and there was a long discussion – there were three or four flashlights and they shone curiously in my face. Amara leaned in through the window and said that I should get out of the car.

'They would like to see what is the matter.'

I was unsure about what was happening, but I was too tired to protest. When I'd gotten out and closed the door two of the young men began rocking the front of the car. They found the clanking sound just behind the left front wheel. The beating the car had taken had finally broken a shock absorber. As I was nodding, listening to Amara's translation of what they were saying to him, boys began scurrying off to the huts. One of the men went to a small truck I could see parked in the shadows.

'They say they will fix it for us,' Amara said, with his quiet acceptance of whatever was happening. But I couldn't see how they could fix it. We had pulled off the edge of a dirt road in an African village in the middle of the night. There wasn't even electricity in the village. In a few moments, however, the boys who had scurried away were clustered again around the car, and the man who had gone to the truck had come back with a jack. Forty-five minutes later, working with flashlights and handtools, they had the car jacked up, the broken shock absorber fixed, and the car back down on the dirt, ready to drive. I didn't know what to say. They had repaired the car with the same kind of noisy spontaneity that had been part of the atmosphere of the dance that I'd begun the day with. There was a note of seriousness as one of the men made a short speech. I waited in the dimness for Amara to translate what he'd said. Most of the flashlights had been turned off to save the batteries. 'He said I should tell you that they didn't have a replacement for the rubber bushing that is part of the shock absorber, and that you should have one put in when you come to a proper garage.' Not knowing what to say I shook the man's hand. I had another discussion with Amara about how much I should pay them. He began again with the ceremonial suggestion that I should decide what I felt it was worth, ending with the practical note that they would be very satisfied with an amount that corresponded to about forty cents in American money. I immediately handed over some tattered bills. The men were, as Amara had said they would be, very satisfied. Flashlights were put on again for a last farewell, hands were shaken all around, and we started again for Banjul.

After we'd traveled a few miles I said to Amara, trying not to sound too surprised, that I didn't know of many places in Europe or the United States where I could come into a small village in the middle of the night and get a car fixed – especially without tools or lights. As with everything else he took it calmly. 'Many of the boys in the village drive trucks. They must know about these things.'

As we drove on I realized that in two days I had seen three different sides of Africa – one the old Africa of slavery and subsistence farming. The second, the village ceremony from the colonial period and the third, the men who had come with their flashlights and fixed the car. They represented the Africa of the future, and it seemed, from the glimpse I'd had, that the future was in secure hands.

9

'The Province Of Freedom'

The countries south of The Gambia and Senegal hadn't been a source of the blues. It was among the musicians of the northern tribes, the griots and the instrumentalists of the kora and the halam, that I'd come the closest to the background of the blues. But I had become interested in everything that I was encountering. In the compounds north of the Gambia River I'd seen a little of modern slavery, but I still had a few questions. I still couldn't put together all the parts of what I had experienced. I decided to go further south, four hundred miles to Sierra Leone, and its port city of Freetown. Thousands of slaves had been freed in the small settlement there and I was curious about the society they'd created. I wanted to see if it had any relationship to the black society I already knew in the United States.

Freetown had been the administrative center for The Gambia as well as Sierra Leone during much of the British colonial period and the traditional way to come to the town was by boat. The airlines scuttling up and down the coast had replaced most of the boat service, though it was still possible to book a passage if you had reliable information and time to wait for the next boat to come along. I took the plane, wanting to see the landscape in the same way that I'd seen it coming over the Sahara. The flight was the same kind of slow, hot drifting that I'd experienced before. Below the plane's small window the coast eddied and swelled behind its broken line of surf. For most of the journey I was flying over a deep, shadowed swamp of mangrove and vines. Across Guinea the land seemed to lose its way in a choked labyrinth of water and plants, and over Liberia there were hundreds of miles where the land was as empty as the Sahara had been, except that here the earth was covered with a thick green blur of vegetation. As the plane came in to the airport several miles north of Freetown in the late afternoon I felt for the first time that I was in a jungle. There was a hanging curtain of leaves on the low hills, the trunks of palms and hard wood trees struggling to lift themselves above it, but finally being swept away in the patterns of shape and intensity that marked the overhanging greeness.

A bus was waiting to take the handful of passengers from the plane to Freetown, but by the time we finished with airport formalities and began the slow drive to the city it was already half dark. We were forced to park on the road and wait in a line of traffic for a ferry to take us across the shadowy expanse of Freetown's bay. It was hot and stuffy in the bus so I scrambled out and walked down to the water. The fading sunset had brought the wind to life, and in the trailing plumes of the approaching darkness, I could feel my hair blown against my sweating forehead, my shirt flattened against my chest as if small hands were patting it to see what there was to the body underneath. I tried to stand up on a low sea wall, but the wind's fitfulness pulled me down from it. In its restlessness the wind was pushing the sea before it in sweeping curves that mounted in hurried surges up the sloping sand. Along the road people were sitting inside their cars with the doors opened, the small lights of their cigarettes flaring up behind the deepening shadows of the windshields.

I could sense scurryings in the dark sand below me, a flurry of activity like the forces driving the wind. I could make out the shapes of land crabs digging into the sand for the night, scuttling sideways down into the slanted openings they had scratched into the sloping beach, then dragging up a clutched heap of sand in the bent crook of a claw. The movement that had caught my eye was the flinging of sand as they scattered it in front of the holes with a sweep of the claw. When I stepped down off the wall and walked toward them they sprang with a straddling sideways motion into the mouths of their half-dug shelters. But – and again I was confronted with the weakness of generalizations; the problem of describing patterns of conduct – one or two of them weren't digging. Through the dusk I could see them edging toward holes the other crabs had labored over, waiting for the crab that was digging to move too far away with a clutch of sand. Then they rushed toward the mouth of the hole and tried to sidle into it. The first crab dropped the sand and scurried back. Scaley claws clattered against scaley claws, the two creatures from another eon stiffened on bent legs in a semi-crouch until the intruder slowly backed off. A moment later he was edging toward another sprayed heap of sand, leaning down into the dark opening, then darting off when a claw inside groped out at the disturbance.

Freetown's harbor was at the base of a high crest of mountains that swelled out of the flat plain I had flown over during the day. The name 'Sierra Leone' means Lion Mountain, and the mountains rose in heavy majesty, in the evening shadows looking as if they had a lion's strength in their coiled shoulders. The city was a ring of lights circling their base. As I stood with my eyes shaded against the wind looking across the bay, a light detached itself from the distant glitter and pushed its swaying reflection out toward us. The ferry, a new German-built vessel, scraped its ways up a cement ramp and opened its white painted mouth to all of us waiting on the road.

When the ferry landed across the bay the string of lights I'd seen in the half darkness became a jammed, deafening jumble of choked streets along the water's edge. I found a bus that was leaving the ferry landing and it forced its way through narrow streets almost impassable with the jams of people. Vendors had flooded over the sidewalks with their small stalls and baskets, and the kerosene lanterns they'd hung up over their merchandise shed a wavering, yellowish light over the tide of faces. Between the worn little stalls, with their piles of fruit, cakes of soap, sun glasses, and canned beans, flowed a sewer with a raised concrete shelving half covering it. On the sewer's shelf women had lined up pans of cooked food, bundles of twigs tied with dried grass, buckets filled with rice. I could see the colored cloth of women's robes everywhere, the reflection of lantern light on bracelets circling bare arms. The bus's horn, squealing like an angry animal, forced an opening ahead of us, and people turned to stare up at us as the bus's sides pressed them back against the filthy walls. Their faces were closed, the expressions sullen and angry. I could see from their features, their costumes, that they came from every tribe in Sierra Leone, and that this jammed street wasn't what they'd come to Freetown to find.

It wasn't what I'd come to find either. The freed slaves in Freetown had created their own society, which had come eventually to be called Creole. The Creoles — with the help of the British — had built the settlement on the slopes of the mountains. These were the people I'd come to see. Above the crowd I could see the houses of old Creole

Freetown. They were built of clapboard or pressed cement blocks, with rows of windows below the roofs to catch the ocean winds. The boards were warped and weathered, the paint was peeling on the cement, but the houses still had a heavy solidity. Lights shone out of the high windows, and I could see waving curtains, like hands trying to attract the attention of someone down on the street. Their faded streamers fluttered out of every window. They were made of lengths of thin flowered cloth – some brighter or newer, some in shreds, but all of them desultorily flapping above our heads as we passed beneath them like flags from a forgotten celebration.

The temperatures of the West African coast haven't changed in the last century, but traveler's attitudes about them have. Now that Europeans and Americans have become so sun-conscious the coastal temperatures are described in travel brochures as 'pleasantly warm', 'sun enriched', or 'invigorating'. Before they were 'cruel', 'inhuman', and always 'unhealthy'. The usual traveler's reaction was like Dobson's account of The Gambia or a more modern description by the correspondent Richard Harding Davis when he visited Sierra Leone in 1908.

> What first impressed me about Sierra Leone was the heat. It does not permit one to give his attention wholly to anything else ... (Davis had made the trip by steam ship and when he landed,) ... We climbed the moss-covered steps to the quay to face a great white building that blazed like the base of a whitewashed stone at white heat. Before it were some rusty cannon and a canoe cut out of a single tree, and seated upon it selling fruit and sun-dried fish, some native women, naked to the waist, their bodies streaming with palm oil and sweat. At the same moment something struck me a blow on the top of the head, at the base of the spine and between the shoulder blades, and the ebony ladies and the white 'factory' were burnt up in a scroll of flame.
>
> I heard myself asking in a far-away voice where one could buy a sun helmet and a white umbrella, and until I was under their protection Sierra Leone interested me no more ...*

The heat still affected me; though I got along with it a little better than Davis was able to. I often wanted to find one of the people who wrote the travel brochures in London or New York and drag them out into the sun at noon and then listen to them try to tell me about 'sun-

* Richard Harding Davis, *The Congo and Coasts of Africa* (London: T. Fisher Unwin, 1908), p. 23.

enriched, balmy tropical temperatures'. I woke up in a shabby, bare hotel room sweating and depressed. I was close to the main street of Freetown in a narrow building filled with narrow corridors and uneven paneling and strips of mirror lining stair landings. By the time I'd reached my room, dragging my bag behind me, I'd felt like I was in a kind of circus labyrinth, only it was silent, and I was the only person there to enjoy it. It was blindingly hot in the streets and I found the ocean air heavy and oppressive after the drier air of the northern coast. Before I'd walked a block my shirt was soaked with sweat and clinging uncomfortably to my back.

The main street itself had a handful of grimy large government buildings and some modern stores, but downhill from it, on the mountain slope leading to the water, there were dreary lines of dark stone houses built on the edges of the littered storm drains. They had all the bleak cheerlessness of the Wesleyan Methodism that had built the town, and except for the heat I could have been on one of the back streets of Glasgow or Aberdeen. My first impressions were similar to those of another of the Victorian travelers, Mary H. Kingsley, who was in Freetown in 1897.

> When you go ashore you will find that most of the stores and houses – the majority of which, it may be remarked, are in a state of acute dilapidation – are of painted wood, with corrugated iron roofs. Here and there, though, you will see a thatched house, its thatch covered with creeping plants, and inhabited by colonies of creeping insects.*

The only addition to the scene was the swarm of cars that choked the streets and tried to force each other out of the way with the metallic fervor of their horn blowing. It was a kind of Gabrieli motet without tuning or rhythm, but with some sort of the same emotionalism.

I could also feel an air of tension around me in the city. People who even stopped to answer questions were guarded and abrupt. They stared at me with unfriendly curiosity. As I walked along one of the winding streets that circled the base of the mountain I realized that there was a stream of people walking in the same direction. Hurrying a little I followed them and suddenly found myself in the middle of a silent crowd that filled the street and sidewalk in front of a walled building. The wall was of bare stucco with a rosette of barbed wire on top of it. A group of men were standing on a corner and I asked them

* Mary Henrietta Kingsley, *Travels in West Africa* (London and New York: Macmillan and Co., Ltd., 1897), p. 16.

what was happening. One of them shrugged,
   'They hanged up some men today. Now they bring them out.'

Five men had been hanged for theft and murder and the crowd was waiting for the bodies to be brought out. In our western societies we are shielded against so much – here was the kind of emotional intensity we usually keep only for sporting events. Everything else is kept at a distance. I could hear groaning, crying in the crowd. Members of the men's families were struggling to get past the line of guards at the door. Policemen waving truncheons suddenly burst out of the prison and forced us away from the two trucks waiting for the bodies. We were shoved forwards and backwards as the police drove us back and the people behind us pressed forward. There was a scream as the first raw wooden box was carried through the door and thrown into the open truck; then the cries stopped. The realization that the bodies were in the hastily made coffins the police were passing out through the crowd silenced us all. Uneasily we parted enough to let the trucks through; then jumped back out of the way as the police hanging from the sides of the trucks began striking at us as they drove off. The guards from the prison itself began dispersing the crowd and the people, still disturbed, gave ground uneasily. In a few moments the road returned to its mid-afternoon torpor and I went nervously back to the main streets of Freetown.

Without the slave trade there probably would have been no modern city of Freetown, but like Banjul it had been established as part of the effort to bring the slave trade to an end. The harbor was first seen by the Portuguese navigator Pedro da Cintra in 1460, who gave the mountains behind the city their name. Over the next two hundred years the harbor was used as a port of call, but there was little trade in slaves. It was difficult to get into the highlands, where most of the tribes lived, and the people of the two dominant groups, the Mende and the Temne, were considered untrustworthy and difficult to deal with. Slavery was just as widespread in the plateau areas as it was everywhere else in West Africa, but the traders weren't interested enough in the slaves from the area to make the extra effort it would have meant to buy them. The ships went on around the bulge of the coastline to what is now Ghana.

The comment that Jobson had made in 1620 when he was offered slaves by one of the rulers along the banks of the Gambia River, that the English 'were a people who did not deale in any such commodities', would seem cynical in the light of England's role in the slave trade in the 18th century, but as the slave trade grew, the opposition to it grew as rapidly and there was a strong abolitionist movement in England working actively to end it. In point of time all of this was distantly remote to the heat and the noise of Freetown's streets as I walked through the city, but it was directly involved with the Creole society that I had come to see.

Freetown was first planned by one of the leaders of the abolitionists, Cecil Sharp, who intended it as a home for slaves freed in Britain. The first group of settlers was sent out in 1787, a mixed collection of freedmen and slaves emancipated after their flight from the American colonies. The place along the harbor where they were landed was called 'The Province of Freedom'. In their distance from Africa Europeans and Americans have often forgotten that Africa was then a land of sharply defined tribal boundaries. It was as hopelessly naive to set a group of freedmen in land controlled by other tribes as it would have been for an 18th century government to set a group of Poles ashore in Sicily and tell them to thrive and be free since they were back in 'Europe'. Within a year disease and attacks by the Temne had all but wiped out the group.

The abolitionists, however, were determined, and they persuaded a native king to lease them a strip of land to develop along the north shore of the peninsula where Freetown now stands. A new settlement was founded, but the attacks continued, both by the tribes and the French, who were now fighting England everywhere in the world. The British government was finally forced to take over the abolitionist's weakened operation in 1808

I could find little from this period left in Freetown. On the main street an old house had been turned into a museum, and its small, jumbled collection was mostly given over to dusty examples of Mende carving. The wooden heads sat on dark shelves gray with dust and neglect. As I went from case to case, looking at the handful of pictures of the early colonial period, at the broken musical instruments and the faded documents, I was followed by school children who were more interested in me than they were in the exhibits themselves. Whenever I turned there was a difference face beside me, looking up and saying, 'You like this? You give me money?' An old, large tree close to the building, its long branches stirring uncomfortably with the traffic slipping past it was described as the 'slave tree' in some of the pamphlets I got from the museum, the place of the old slave market in Freetown. Since Freetown was probably the only coastal town for thousands of miles where the sale of slaves was of negligible importance the description seemed a little forced. But it was certainly an old tree and it had marked one end of the main street during the town's first years of existence.

The Creole society I had come to see had also come out of this period of English involvement with the area. The members of the different tribes and the freedmen who had been landed at Freetown turned to English as a common language and a dialect called 'krio' or 'pidgin' or simply 'Creole' developed. It is still the dominant language in the coastal settlements, recognizably English, but so altered and adapted to the local environment that an English speaker new to the country has to learn it as a separate language. English law was the legal base of the community and it was a center of missionary activity, especially since most of the freedmen, who had spent their early lives as slaves, were already Christian.

In 1807, the year before the British took over some of the essential government functions, the whole process of growth in the small settlement was speeded up. In that year the British declared the slave trade illegal and stationed a naval squadron off the coast at Freetown to pursue and capture slave ships. A court of the Vice-Admiralty was set up in Freetown, and suddenly it began to have an importance reaching up and down the slave coast. The first slaver was captured the next year. In 1815, when all of Europe abolished slavery the squadron was expanded and the 'Courts of Mixed Commission' were also set up to deal with the suddenly illegal trading.

It was lonely, arduous sea duty trying to apprehend the slavers, since they had the whole coast line to hide in, and the local Africans who controlled the trade had no intention of giving it up. To continue the sales they turned to ship captains willing to work outside the law, and the slave trade – always brutal and degrading – became even more cruel and lawless. But once England had made the decision it continued to abide by it, and its ships doggedly patrolled thousands of miles of ocean, trying to run down ships carrying cargoes of slaves. England had been a dominant factor in the slave trade, and its ships and land forces had helped keep the trade alive for two centuries, but it is one of the ironies of history that when the decision was made to end it, England probably sacrificed more men and more effort in the struggle than it had in all the years before.

But once a slaver had been captured, and its crew and cargo hauled into Freetown, what could the British do with them? The ships were eventually released, and the crews finally freed, but what could be done with the slaves? They couldn't be returned to where they'd come from. Usually they'd been brought hundreds of miles overland before they were loaded onto ships and the European control in Africa extended only to a few tiny coastal areas. All the rest was in the hands of local chiefs and kings, and any freed slaves passing through their territory would simply be seized and sold again. Even if the original homes of the slaves were only a few hundred miles from Freetown there was no way for them to cover those few hundred miles. So the British simply released them. Most of them were freed in Freetown, although others were also freed on the land the British had bought at Banjul, in The Gambia. Each year hundreds, sometimes thousands, of slaves found themselves in Sierra Leone, suddenly part of a black society composed of other ex-slaves, involved in a complicated relationship with a British colonial government. It was these newly freed men and women who became the Creoles.

As I walked the streets I could understand why I had felt, the first night, the difference between the people filling the streets and the old houses behind them. It was the Creoles who had built the older sections of Freetown, and it was the inland people who were moving into the city now. The voices I heard were speaking Mende or Temne, not Creole, with its rhythmic, English-like sound. It had always been a town of shops and shop keepers. Mary H. Kingsley, in 1897, found the streets already lined with small commercial establishments.

The shops, which fringe these streets in an uneven line, are like rooms with one side out, for store-fronts, as we call them, are here unknown. Their doors are generally raised on a bed of stone a little above street level, but except when newly laid, these stones do not show, for the grass grows over them, making them into green banks. Inside the shops are lined with shelves, on which are placed bundles of gay-colored Manchester cottons and shawls, Swiss clocks, and rough but vividly colored china; or — what makes a brave show — brass, copper, and iron cooking pots. Here and there you come across a baker's, with trays of banana fritters of tempting odor; and there is no lack of barbers and chemists ...*

I spent most of the evenings out in the streets walking along the lines of shops and stalls. There were glaringly bright overhead lights that cast elaborate shadows across the fronts of the buildings, turning the sloping sewer troughs the women straddled into black pits below the legs of their playing children. The air was smoky from the small kerosene flames the women lit on the battered cartons where they spread out the things they had to sell. No one spoke to me, or even glanced my way. If we had tried to speak we wouldn't have been able to hear each other over the tinny roar of music that blared out of the neon squared windows of the record shops. I had already learned that most of the early Creole music had been swept aside by the tide of newer tribal music coming down to the coast, and then the popular forms of African popular music had largely replaced them both. There were some Creole songs, I was told, a little dance music in some of the settlements, but there were only a few older people keeping it alive.

Even though I didn't expect to find any traces of the blues I was still interested in Creole music, but it certainly hadn't become part of the modern Sierra Leone culture. The hours of tribal music that I'd heard on the radio in Senegal and The Gambia, the traditional ballads and the kora playing, were confined to their own areas. What I heard here was African popular music, heavily influenced by American Soul and Jamaican Reggae styles. I was curious why the Creoles hadn't created a distinct musical culture, as slaves from some of the same tribes had done in the United States. The people I asked were confused by the question. 'But there has always been so much music here,' one man protested, and I understood what he was saying. The Creoles, when they were freed in Sierra Leone, encountered musical cultures and traditions that

* Kingsley, *Travels*, p. 17.

weren't so much different from their own. There wasn't the gulf that had separated African tribal music from the European music forms that the slaves had found in America. There, as slaves and then as Americans of African descent, they were forced to remain outside the white society — they had to create a music that was distinctly their own. Here, they hadn't been isolated, despite the hostility of the local tribes. Their music had simply evolved, along with the other musical styles along the coast, and become blended into the new African melting pot. For most of my stay in Freetown I left the tape recorder in its case under the bed in my room.

All of the shops were open in the evenings. Beside the record shops were the tailors with their blue lights ('Diploma from London'), the photographers with their ancient cameras and displays of fading portraits, the men in small door openings bent over the painted black knuckles of their sewing machines. The atmosphere was stifled and watchful, even if no one was paying attention to me. Mary H. Kingsley had found a mood that was generally casual and relaxed, but even then there had been signs of another reality. For most of the shops,

> ... There is usually a counter across the middle, over which customers and casual callers alike love to loll. Some brutal tradesmen, notably chemists, who presumably regard this as unprofessional, affix tremendous nails; with their points outwards, to the fronts of their counter tops, in order to keep their visitors at a respectful distance ...*

In the new Freetown, theft had become so widespread that most of the small corner shops that sold food and cigarettes had heavy wire mesh screens covering everything for sale. A small opening was left in the mesh for a hand to reach in with money, and a hand inside to pass out what had been bought. To keep the hand reaching in from taking anything else the opening inward was shaped like a fish trap, with a tunnel drawn out of the wire mesh so that the groping hand met only strands of wire.

I spent so much time in the streets because the drabness of the hotel room made it impossible to stay inside. The walls were splotched and peeling, and the door had been broken in so many times that there was

*Kingsley, *Travels*, p. 17.

no way to lock it. If I turned on the large, rusty fan in the center of the room it jerked like a seagull flapping toward a beach. Lying under it I felt that a whole mewing flock of seagulls was trying to find a place to land around me. If I turned off the fan and the bare, dangling bulb I was left to the whine of the mosquitoes and the noise of voices in the corridors. Even though I was on the fourth floor the fear of theft was so omnipresent that there were bars over the window. The poverty that choked the streets had a more human dimension than the distant threat I felt in my room, and I could see in the faces along the streets some of the disorientation I felt as I walked the streets and tried to find my own bearings in the noise and confusion.

It was almost as difficult to sort out the ambiguities of the Creoles' position in the society of their own country. Since they'd already been separated from their tribal cultures they were dependent on the British in their struggle to build a new social and economic structure. Missionary groups flocked to Freetown – one of the bleakest buildings among the rows of stone houses close to the water was the Methodist Church – and they brought a degree of schooling with them, along with their tracts and their prejudices. Creoles soon had become useful to the British in offices and in lower level administrative positions. Freetown was responsible for the administration of the British trade areas in The Gambia and the Gold Coast – now Ghana – and as more and more territory came under the British protectorate status the need for clerks and managers grew. To train the people they needed, the British founded Fourah Bay College, which was finally built on some level ground on the mountainside above Freetown.

At an earlier moment in history there had been a group of Arab scholars living and teaching in Timbuktoo, on the Niger, but after the city was razed by the Moroccans the centers of learning were never rebuilt; so Freetown's college was the only advanced educational institution in all of West Africa. In the mid-19th century it was of considerable importance in creating a native administrative class. It represented, of course, a kind of cultural assimilation that destroyed the last vestiges of the Creoles' tribal identities, but the only other alternative for the British was to abandon them on the narrow strip of land they'd bought on the side of the mountain and let them fend for themselves. Since the Creoles had already been enslaved by other tribes the alternative was worse than anything that could happen to them in the struggling colony.

This led, however, to increasing friction between the Creoles and the native tribes, who were becoming uneasily aware that the small settlement they'd ceded land to was growing into a major port. The British, in fact, were steadily extending the boundaries of their colony by local treaties and the purchase of tracts of land. The Creoles, who as ex-slaves would have gone to the bottom of African society, instead were becoming increasingly influential, and were taking over positions where they had a small measure of authority over some areas of responsibility between the tribes and the British. They were better educated, better able to deal with Europeans, and they had acquired a level of sophistication that bewildered and angered the tribal chieftains. If the tribal leaders had been able to withstand the lure of the technology that the Europeans introduced there would have been little trouble, but they were irresistibly drawn to what they could see of European culture, and when they came close what they encountered were the Creoles. Their growing irritation finally led to bloody uprisings against missionaries, traders, and the Creoles in the 1890s. In the first outbreak of rage some men of the tribes even murdered any of their own children who had learned English, and it was only with the arrival of British naval forces that the killing was stopped.

I spoke to one of the older Creoles who was working in one of the offices in the city and he felt that despite the difficulties the Creoles were facing what was happening to them was in some ways just.

> The Creoles in those days were so arrogant, you have no idea, and arrogant is the word to use for it. They had learned some English and they could do mathematics, the little they'd been taught, and that put them so far ahead of everybody else. They were everywhere you turned, doing all the jobs for the British all over the colony. Not only this colony but the other colonies along the whole coast of Africa. The jobs weren't so much, just clerks or bookkeepers, perhaps, but they let it go to their heads. Now – what can I say about it? We have reaped what our fathers sowed, though that's a bit hard on our fathers, who didn't think things would ever change. But things have changed. Everything has changed from the way it was when I was a boy. So now we have to pay a little. But I don't think it's all bad. I think it had to

become more even for everyone in the country – and I think there will still be a place for the Creole when all of this is over.

In 1896 the British established a protectorate over the inland areas and began a desultory development program that yielded very little result until the discovery of diamonds in 1931. Diamonds and iron ore became the colony's two leading exports, even though the British had given the mineral concessions to British firms at terms that were ruinous to the colony itself. When independence came in 1963, one of the first acts of the new government was to try to get back some share of the wealth of the country. There was intense resentment toward the British, and it extended to the Creoles, who had been so closely associated with the old way of life. It was a grim irony that in Sierra Leone it had been an advantage to have been a slave.

When the country achieved independence, the Creoles were still needed for jobs on every level of government, but there was so much resentment at their position in Freetown that the government began giving jobs on the basis of tribal background. To give the jobs to the best qualified candidates almost always meant giving the job to a Creole. What did they think about this? The man I'd talked to in the town itself was educated, in the civil service, and he was old enough to be philosophic about the difficulties. It was much more difficult for people further down the social scale, and I could see that it would be difficult for younger men and women. I realized that the only way I could find out more of their own feelings about their experience was to find some way to get a closer glimpse of their lives. I wasn't interested in the middle-class families who lived like Europeans in newer houses up on the mountainsides. I was still trying to come closer to their consciousness of slavery and I thought I could find it in the small Creole villages scattered along the coast and high on the steep slopes above Freetown. I decided to try the villages above me; since they were stretched along the winding road that continued past Fourah Bay College, and I knew I could get a taxi to take me there. I waited for a day that was less blindingly hot, but finally realized, looking at the flat, sluggish surface of the bay with the baleful ball of the sun hunched over it, that there wouldn't be any cooler days, so I put some notes and cheese and bread into my shoulder bag and started for the villages.

10

A Creole Village

Taxi drivers are difficult to deal with throughout West Africa. Prices are arbitrary and the occasional European or American riding with one of them represents a chance to make up for dozens of local passengers paying three or four cents to ride a mile with a bundle of wood, two baskets of nuts, and a string of still gasping fish. The first rule is to set a price before you get into the taxi. You expect to pay three or four times more than an African would have to pay, but you're still determined to get the price down to at least half of what the driver first asked. In most countries along the coast when the arguing's over you can get in and forget about it until you get where you want to go. In Sierra Leone the arguing never stopped.

As always, I asked first in the shops what I should expect to pay for a taxi. There were the usual smiles and a shrug, 'For you ...', a careful suggestion that I was going to have to pay more. A glance at me to see if I was conscious of this. I was. A nod of understanding, 'Don't pay more than ...'. A little anxiously; since if the driver got a lot out of me he might try to get it out of someone who actually lived in Freetown. I had already learned in other places that it didn't do much good to try to go from driver to driver. It just meant even more arguing since I had to argue with the first driver at the same time as I was trying to arrange a price with the second.

On the street, the moment I stepped off the curb and looked around, a taxi appeared from the other side of a wagon selling plastic combs and sunglasses. The usual large, unconvincing car, with an unhappy rattle to it. The driver was short and watchful, and his eyes studied me suspiciously when, instead of getting in, I went to his side of the taxi and told him where I wanted to. A simple beginning. He knew where it was; 'A long way.' It wasn't so far, I said, and he looked at me even more suspiciously. When I asked for the price he named a sum that would have kept a family alive in Freetown's shanty areas for two days. I offered a price slightly below what I had been told was the usual fare. Anger from the driver. A short heated description of all the major food items that had to be purchased for a man and his children, and their prices. When I insisted on a price slightly above the usual fare his expression changed from anger to sorrow, we reached a compromise somewhere in the middle and he motioned for me to get in.

Usually this would have been enough, but for a Sierra Leone driver it wasn't. Twice the taxi shuddered to a stop on the winding road up the dry slope and we discussed money again. At the edge of town he'd picked up two more passengers and they had settled on a price about one-fourth of what I was to pay, and when we finally reached the first building of the College he held out his hand to me for his money; then held out his hand for money from the two Africans, who understood what he was doing. He held up what I had paid and what they had paid so I could see the difference – we didn't have enough of a language in common to do much more than this – and smiled at me. Since I had at least arrived at the place I had set out for I could only smile back, and we left each other with fixed, nodding grins as he rattled further up the mountain to the center of the College buildings.

The College itself was on a series of small shelves on the side of the mountain, its white buildings on bare stretches of brown, dry earth and irregular plantings. The hallways of the buildings were empty and cool. I'd come during a school holiday. It looked like dozens of community colleges in the western United States – except for the wide, stretching view that opened out below the buildings and the dry look of the landscape. A girl in one of the school offices suggested I go to a Creole village on top of the mountain. I could get up to it in an hour.

There were taxis standing under the sparse trees, but I couldn't force myself to go through another argument. I sat on a stone, out of the heat, and ate the food I'd put in my bag. The sun was stifling hot, but the air wasn't as oppressively heavy as it was down below. I could walk up to the village, and have some feeling of what it meant to be on the top of the mountain; since at the time the Creoles built their houses there was no way to get up to the village except by foot. The road twisted and wound up the harsh slope, as though it were pulling itself up the mountain hand over hand, reaching up to pull at the loop of tar above it as it clambered upward. The little level land on the mountain shoulder was mostly used for the homes of the College teaching staff.

They lived in neat stucco houses with brilliantly flowering gardens set back off the road. As I climbed higher the view below me became even more spectacular – the streets of Freetown, white and shining in the sun, the pale, unblinking eye of the water, the distant line of haze marking the other side of the bay. I stopped often to look down; the drop so precipitous that it seemed like a pebble would drop straight down to the streets thousands of feet below if you simply leaned out a little and tossed it off.

Ahead of me two boys in school uniform were also walking up the road, carrying cloth school bags that they shifted from hand to hand as they climbed. I caught up with them and spoke to them in English, thinking they were from Creole families. They answered in careful school English that they were members of the Loko tribe, and the village I was going to was divided between the Creoles and the Lokos. I fell back again and walked behind them first over a rounded crest and then into a rough area of cut-over jungle that was a jumble of small trees, vines, and choking bushes. There was a control post on the road, checking cars going down through it to the College. The road climbed past it through a steadily thickening jungle growth toward a stubbled peak rising behind it.

How impossible it must have been for the first slave families who climbed up the slope to try to make some kind of life on the hard, leached earth! They couldn't raise much on the steep mountainside, there wasn't much to hunt. If there had been no place for them in the development of the Colony they would have had to stay in their mountain villages, picking at the poor ground, trying to make it yield a life for them. I began passing the first houses, ramshackle wooden clapboard buildings like the ones I'd seen in the older sections of Freetown. They resembled European wooden cottages, but they'd been built out of whatever timber was available and the lines of clapboard were warped and uneven. They were brightly painted in oranges and greens, though many of them were deeply weathered and the old paint was only there as a summer reminiscence. The ground around them had been planted with flowering bushes that reached up to the windows from the trampled bare patches of earth.

I couldn't see many people at first, only the laboriously cleared patches of garden that trailed down the slopes beside the houses. Far below, in the jungle off the edge of the ridge, patches of land had been cut back and planted, like a green slash on the side of the mountain. The houses were scattered through the jungle, only their clapboard sides visible through the screen of leaves. I couldn't see faces at the windows, and curtains hung slackly in the afternoon silence. Through the tops of the trees to the south were distant lines of mountains, their harsh lines of ridge beginning to soften in the afternoon haze. This must have been a final sad irony for the village's people. Most of the freed slaves had come originally from the Gold Coast and Nigeria, and it must have seemed possible for them to stand on the mountain top and look toward the lands they'd come from. In the first years they probably spent long hours staring off toward the wavering line of earth that might have been their homes.

At a small board house near the edge of the scattered village I found two teen-age boys sitting on an unpainted veranda. They got to their feet when I came toward them, speaking school English instead of Creole.

'Everybody working now. You want to come back? If you come back people will be here.'

I looked back along the road. There was nowhere to stop in the village. Most of the houses were empty, and everyone seemed to be off somewhere. They wouldn't come back for hours.

'Everybody has supper; they will come home then.' The boys were still standing stiffly beside the house, and I realized that if I stayed I would only make the handful of people I'd seen more uncomfortable. I told them I'd come later – at the end of the afternoon – and went back along the road, down through the stretch of jungle I'd laboriously climbed past an hour before, down to the small white shapes of the College buildings pressed against the unrelenting slide of the mountain.

I decided that I would try to record any Creole songs I could find in the village, and I spent the afternoon laying out batteries and plugs. When the sun finally sank below the ridge I put a notebook into my canvas bag, picked up the recording equipment, and went outside to look for a taxi to take me. More arguments, the usual alternations of anger and self-pity, finally a shrug, and we lurched off. But this time the roads were empty. No one else wanted to go up; so his fare was only what I was paying him. Halfway to the village the driver pulled off the road, threatening to leave me. More arguments. A long discussion on the price of a bag of rice. The price for the ride went up. We started again. The driver was younger, thin and nervous, with uneven, gapped teeth and a wrinkled white shirt. Beyond the College the arguing started again, and finally I was left at the first houses of the village, the shouting voice of the driver fading down the road like the sounds on a dying radio, strident but incoherent as they dissipated into the air.

I could see that the people were back in the village now. There were voices coming from the yards, the soft light of kerosene lamps shone through some of the windows. I could see faces, feel the presence of people on the shaded porches. The two boys hadn't expected me to come back, but they were still in the yard of the house where I'd first seen them. They had said they could take me to find older people who knew a little about their history, about the village itself. The three of us went a hundred yards back along the road and climbed wooden steps up the earth back to a small, crowded house compound. There were four houses facing in to the littered patch of bare ground between them. It was a kind of half compromise between the African village compound, with the houses enclosed behind walls, and the European village, with its houses lining a street.

There were people sitting outside the house doors on homemade stools or old wooden crates. They suggested a young woman further down the road when I asked about songs. Most of the village people followed me as I went to find her. She laughed shyly and agreed to sing a few lullabies. She was round-faced and pretty, and sang in a low, soft voice. Everyone agreed that there wasn't a great deal of music left in the village: 'That was in our father's time.' When I asked them about their life today they talked hesitantly, but with a deep consciousness of their position in the new Sierra Leone. It was the hopelessness of the distances that had turned them to the British. They knew that they were from Nigeria, as most of the people in the group remembered from parents and grandparents, but in the missionary schools in Freetown they'd seen their first maps of Africa, and Nigeria was a thousand miles away. The school boys seemed more ready to talk about the history.

'We came to Leicester by slave trade. Those people that lived along the coast and were captured by slave trade. Then they entered into Sierra Leone. When we came settlers was living in the town so they decided to find places for us. So they decided to send us to the villages. Some of the governors they give the villages names from they own name, like Leicester, Gloucester, Regency, Willberforce, Charles. That was Williams Willberforce, he give his name to Willberforce village, and Leicester village during that time was founded, and it was the first village that was founded.'

Did anyone remember what tribe they had come from. 'No,' slowly, thoughtfully, from the young woman who had been singing children's songs for me. After a silence, one of the school boys again.

'Some of us, we are Nigerian. We know that. Some of us are Nigerian in fact. Our forefathers were captured along the coast in the ships and we were taken to Freetown, and some of us, due to civilization, we became Creole.'

But there was unease, discomfort, as we talked. Not towards me, but toward the situation they were being forced into.

'Tribalism is the bad thing now. It's tribalism the only thing keeps us down.'

For them the last rising of the inland tribes, in 1896, was still recent, still a cloud on the horizon. It was only the British Navy that had stopped the slaughter then. If it were to happen now the British wouldn't be there to help, and with the modern tribal massacres in Nigeria and Burundi still raw in their memory they felt the tribal threat hanging over them. Tribalism, the struggle to maintain their Christianity, their concerns were different from those of other people I'd talked to – except in their universal worry over the price of rice. The voices rose in the soft, song-like speech. I asked if they felt an identification with other ex-slaves – the black men and women of the United States.

'The black people in the United States, are they African or American?'

There was an abrupt answer from a younger man sitting on the edge of a porch, 'African.'

The other people sitting on the porch turned to look at him. He was strong faced, in a red short sleeved shirt and cotton shorts. He had a job in Freetown, I learned later, and the others gave him a kind of precedence. He looked nervously down at the ground, then carefully added,

'But they been gone so long, they be Americans now.'

What did he mean that they were Americans now?

'It's customs. The customs they have are American. You tell what people are by their customs and these people, when we see them, the American black people, they have American customs. They come to Freetown, and they don't come up here to stay with us, even if we are the same people in the beginning. They stay down in Freetown, in the hotel there, and when they talk to us they only think of us as waiters or taxi drivers or people in a shop. They have the customs of Americans, and they couldn't live our life now.'

What about the Creoles? They didn't have any of the customs of their own tribes. They were as disoriented as the Americans of African descent.

'We don't have the customs of any tribe, it is true. But the customs we have are African. Even if we have changed and it don't be like the tribe we came from, what we have in our own customs it's African, because we still live here. We still are part of Africa. Africa is very large and it have many people and they all have their own customs, and we have our own customs as Creole people. So that make us African, though we are a little different.'

But since they, too, had moved away from a tribal structure in their lives could they feel, in some way, a sense of identity with Americans who had been slaves? I had learned that one of the realities of slavery is that its cultural dislocation has a longer and more destructive effect than the loss of physical freedom. The only way I could make the question clear was to ask, 'Are the American black men brothers?' There was an uncomfortable stir of laughter at the question.

'No.' The answer coming slowly. 'They not be brothers to us here.'

It grew darker. Most of the people had gone back into their houses. A young woman was sitting on the steps talking to the schoolboys. I crossed the yard with two of the men and we sat together on the railing of the porch outside the room of the man in the red shirt who had answered the questions about their feelings toward black Americans. He was sitting across from me, and I could see into the door of his room. It was a bare wooden opening with a bed, a box for his possessions, clothes hanging from a string, a small table covered with cans and pictures and an old clock. He was thoughtful for a moment, and then asked,

'What about racism in America?'

He wanted to know about the laws, the restrictions, the attitudes, I could tell him about what was changing, what had changed, what was resisting change. As we talked I was conscious that he did have a feeling of identification with black Americans, even though he'd denied this kind of bond earlier. It was as if his feeling of alienation from the tribal societies around him had given him – and the other men who were sitting in the shadows listening and nodding – a consciousness of the American whose background was African. It was the first time along the African coast that I'd felt this consciousness. The man questioning me about the possibilities of advancement in rank for a black man in the United States Army was the first African I'd met who was concerned with his racial identity. The men and women I'd talked to in other sections of the coast had seemed almost unconcerned with their identity as Africans. It was only the people who had become detribalized, whether it was here in Leicester Village or in an American black ghetto, who had a concept of themselves structured out of their racial consciousness.

As we talked I could feel their confusion at the loss of the British presence in Sierra Leone. The Creoles had supported independence, but their closest identification had been with the British that they served so well. It wasn't a surprise, in reading Richard Wright's description of his trip to Ghana, to learn that the first African he talked to on the boat, the Chief Justice of Nigeria who was – in the period just before the first wave of independence – convinced that Africans weren't ready for self-rule, was a Freetown Creole. The freed slaves in Freetown and the villages around it had had a long and involved relationship with the British. The man I was sitting with was talking about the church in Freetown, and its work with the schools, and another man sitting beside us broke in suddenly and said,

'The English gave us an education and thank God for that!'

I had come very close to the heart of this small settlement alone on its hump of mountain above the darkening ocean. We talked for a few more moments, desultorily. We had said everything we could say to each other. The men stood up and stretched. It was only a little after nine, but it was late for people who got up with the sun. The houses around us were dark, with only an occasional yellowish square of light behind the sway of the inevitable curtains at the window – a last kerosene lamp still burning. We shook hands in the shadows of the porch. The two boys I'd met first were still sitting on the steps waiting for me and we walked together to the edge of the village. They wanted to know if there were some way they could go on with their schooling when the school in Freetown ended. I didn't know. I could only tell them that there must be some way, since I'd met people who had gone on, who had left their small villages and then come back. The boys left me in the stillness, calling goodbye in their best school English as I started back down the winding road to the bay.

At the College there was a taxi idling close to the door of the kitchen. He was waiting for two of the kitchen helps so he could take them down to Freetown. It was too late for arguments. I simply reached in his window with as much money as I thought the trip should cost. He took it without protest, and we sat in the car's softly rattling darkness. The two women came out of the kitchen, got into the taxi without glancing toward me, and in silence we twisted our way down the mountainside to the empty streets.

11

The African Blues Roots

As I began to pack up the tapes and notes the next morning after I'd come down from the Creole village I realized that I had looked as far as I could for the sources of the blues. If I were to continue recording in The Gambia or Senegal I might find other versions of the same songs, or slightly different instrumental examples, but I already had a broad outline of what I would find. I could only fill in a few of the details. If I were to continue further south along the coast I could encounter music that had also come over to the American South, but it wouldn't have much connection to the blues. It was time to sort out what I had found.

I had two days to wait before I could get a plane back to The Gambia. The air-conditioner whined with such strong protests that I couldn't hear over it, I propped the window open in the room to get some air, and set the tape recorder up under the mosquito netting. The tapes I'd recorded were scattered over the bed and on the floor where I could lean down and pick them up. It was clear, as I had first realized listening to the griot songs, that they didn't sound much like the blues. The two song forms came from different musical idioms. But I could also hear certain traits – like the way of singing and the rhythmic texturing – that were common to each of them. At some point they had perhaps sounded much more alike, but both the griot's music and the music in the southern United States had changed, each of them going in their own directions. The voices themselves had a great deal of similarity in tone and texture. If a griot like Jali Nyama Suso had sung in English the sound of his voice would have been difficult to distinguish from an Afro-American singer's. There was the same kind of tone production, same forcing of higher notes. In the gruffness of the lower range and the strong expressiveness of the middle voice I could hear stylistic similarities to singing I had heard in many parts of the South.

The differences came in the structure of the melodies and the accompaniments that the griots played. At first some of the songs I had recorded had seemed almost formless, but as I listened more closely I could hear the structural elements that gave them their unity. I could begin to describe the griots' songs. Melodically they were built from a long, lyric line that introduced the subject of the text. As the singer went on he half-sang, half-chanted the new verses, sometimes saying a great deal in a short space of the song, and in the new verses he continued to suggest the outline of the original melody he had started with. There was always a feeling of the lyric opening that gave the song its individual character. I could best characterise it for myself by thinking of it as a kind of set of variations on a melody, but the variations were shaped by the words of the text, and not by melodic embellishments. When I listened again to songs of Jali Nyama's like 'Kelefa Ba', which he said was one of the oldest in his repertoire, I could sense the melody, even in the middle of a long narrative passage.

Some of the songs had an A-B form. There was a kind of refrain that alternated with the narrative verses. The song 'Chedo' was structured in this way. There was considerably less variation in the refrains, although sometimes they also had inserted textual materials that gave a new contour to the melodic line. The refrains, and the phrases of the songs themselves, were generally clear and simple – they had a form that was easy to remember after a few hearings, and their simplicity helped hold together the 'variations' in the melodies that came later. Older griots I had recorded, like Jali Nyama's uncle Falie Kuyateh, used considerably less elaboration in their songs, and some of the simple dance pieces they performed used one or two melodies over and over again.

There was no harmonic change in the accompaniments played on the kora or the balafon. The backgrounds were built of short, repetitive rhythmic units. The units were usually in a duple meter – nothing that I heard was in a triple meter. There wasn't a close integration between the sung rhythm and the accompaniment rhythm. They functioned as a kind of complement to each other, but at the same time they were dependent on each other since each song had its own unique accompaniment. It was clear that – as in almost all African music – there was a conscious avoidance of a rhythmic stress that came in both the voice and the accompaniment at the same moment. In all of the songs there was a subtle rhythmic texturing. The accompaniments themselves had a multileveled texture, achieved with the thumb and the fingers setting up different rhythms. This was easier to do with the kora than on the halam, but the halam players did it with beats on the skin of the instrument.

To follow the patterns of this rhythmic texturing I began making diagrams on the back pages of my notebook. One of the typical accompaniment figures was the pattern that Jali Nyama used for the song 'Kalefa Ba'. It was in a duple meter, 8/4, and the thumb stroke was almost completely regular. The alteration came in the last beat. He left a pause, and then played a shorter note as an 8th note anticipation of the next 8/4 pattern. This use of a 'pick-up' note helped clarify the rhythm and also gave the singer a point of reference in his performance. If I had to characterise the level of complexity of the finger pattern I would say that it's carefully constructed to give a sense of syncopation and stress alteration, but at the same it's kept simple enough so that the whole pattern is still clear and easily followed.

In his accompaniment for 'Chedo' the rhythm in the fingers was less elaborate, and the thumb had a delayed entrance, syncopating the whole pattern. Here it's the fingers that play the anticipatory 8th note, as the pattern begins again.

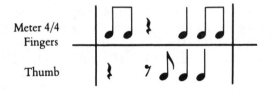

As I had already found, there was no harmonic change in the accompaniment, but for 'Kalefa Ba', the kora was played in a major mode, and in a minor mode for 'Chedo'.

This, in simple outline, was the kind of music I had heard from the griots. Did it have any relationship to the blues? On the surface they didn't seem to have much in common. One of the characteristics of the country blues styles – the oldest blues, and because of that, presumably the closest to the African background – is the close integration between the melody played on the guitar and the voice, which is quite unlike the African accompaniments. In the songs of Mississippi musicians like Charley Patton or Son House the guitar was often used to state the melodic phrase. The first note of a line was played on the guitar, and the guitar finished the line in response to the melody sung by the voice. In the bottleneck style the guitar and the voice sometimes stated the melody in unison while the rhythm was reiterated by the thumb on the guitar's lower strings.

Part of this could be explained by the fact that the guitar and the kora or the halam have different sound characteristics. The guitar can sustain a tone longer; so melodic effects that are impossible on the African instruments can be played on the blues instrument. With the guitar for accompaniment the blues musicians can play and sing at a slower tempo. When I looked at southern banjo music, however, which was certainly closer in style to African sources since the instrument was the New World's version of the halam, I did find the same kind of repeated rhythmic figures. Sadly the era of recording began after the banjo had largely been taken over by white performers, but in the recordings by older artists like Gus Cannon, who played the banjo, there was a much closer similarity in style.

There was another kind of southern blues music, though, that seemed to have a closer relationship. All of the older singers had a repertoire of faster dance pieces, which seemed to antedate the classic guitar blues. Some of the pieces I'd recorded years before with the Mississippi singer Big Joe Williams – songs that we gave names to like 'Levee Break Blues' or 'This Heavy Stuff of Mine', had this looser structure. The accompaniments were flailing repetitive rhythmic patterns, and the voice was only loosely connected to the pulse of the guitar. One piece I'd recorded with the Louisiana singer Robert Pete Williams, 'Goin' Out Have Myself a Ball', had almost no harmonic change at all – and in modern blues playing there have been a number of bands who play long improvisatory pieces without harmonic change.

What I found more interesting than the lack or presence of harmonic changes was the obvious use of rhythmic texturing – the same kind of texturing that was characteristic of the griot music and certainly has left its imprint on every other African musical style. Despite the simplicity of the blues structure and the obviousness of its harmonic changes there is considerable variation within the form. When I was first annotating blues melodies I found it almost impossible to find the place in the rhythm where the voice began singing – even though the starting place for the line was clearly stated in the guitar accompaniment. What I realized, after some years of struggle, was that the singers were consciously avoiding a simultaneous stressed rhythmic accent in both the guitar and the voice, and I soon found that the shifts of accent had their own musical characteristics. One aspect of the blues style that had always fascinated me – the anticipation of the harmonic change by the voice before the harmony shifts in the guitar – I realized now was another aspect of this rhythmic building. The loud foot tapping that had plagued so many of the early recording engineers was also part of this complex texturing of the rhythmic pattern. Some of the pieces I had recorded with Big Joe Williams had almost been constructed around the heavy tapping of his foot.

It was clear, I felt, as I lay in the stifling hotel room listening to tapes, stretched out on the sagging bed with the noises from the street drifting in the window, that the two styles of music were different from each other – but still I could find things that suggested a relationship. Structurally the two forms were hardly related at all. The blues is built on a strophic model and one popular form of the twelve bar blues has become so fixed as a pattern that it has become a definition of the blues itself. The use of rhyme, the controlled line lengths – the use of the repeated two lines that begin a blues verse – these are all things that separate the blues from its African sources. Certainly the subject material has little relationship – and obviously reflects the social rank of the singers. The griots were the entertainers of kings and wealthy merchants, and their songs were concerned with the history of the people of the tribe or the family. The blues singers, who were part of a minority systematically excluded from a significant role in their society, used little history and even less political comment. The blues function in American black society as a popular love song – in the early period almost obsessively concerned with infidelity. This certainly seems to have been a metaphor for more deeply hidden emotional attitudes, but as a kind of song it is much more limited than the griot narratives, with their sweep of history and personal commentary on the people involved in the distant events.

The blues as we know it, however, is to an extent a creation of the recording industry, and there seems to have been a freer use of narrative away from the recording microphones. Robert Pete Williams came to mind again; since he created many blues that were much more freely structured. I thought in particular of his 'blues' telling of his arrest and imprisonment for murder in 1956. As he had sung it for me in 1976 it had some of the style of the narratives I'd heard from the Mandingo singers.

> ... Locked me down, they tried me for my life,
> April the 6th, 1956, they sent me to Angola.
> Not to lie, not to lie, they tried me for my life.
> Cried, let's keep the poor boy.
>
> You know I called out, you cannot keep me, no, no,
> I said I got a man in here in this courthouse with all power in his hand.
> They asked me what man that you talkin' 'bout,
> I was lookin' dead down at the Bible you know,
> I said God above got all power over me.
>
> Yeh, you got to send me to your pen, I ain't thinkin'
> 'bout your 'lectric chair at all.
> Oh you got to send me to your pen, and I'm not be there long.
> Oh yeh, you got to send me to your pen Lord, I'm not goin' be there long ...

There are some similarities in style between a song like this and a griot performance, but the subject matter is completely different. Even a singer from a small village outside of Banjul sang about kings and the battles between empires. A song by Falie Kuyateh began,

> Give the Tirimangs the guns to fight with.
> Oh, the people of Tirimang
> Give the bows and arrows to the Tarawalles
> of the Tirimang family, the fearless people
> who are always ready,
> the families of the Tirimang.
> Always give them the bows and arrows to fight with.
> Always give them the bows and arrows to fight with.

> It is God who helps every man,
> It is not men who can help themselves ...

So I had found some things that related the two musical forms – the style of singing, the occasional use of rhythmic figures, the kind of texturing of the voice and accompanying rhythm. Also the role of the singers in their small communities were similar, and in the rural areas of the South a blues man performed a much wider range of songs than recordings would suggest. They were their farm's dance band, children's entertainer, gospel singer, and blues man, all rolled into one. The usual name for them was 'songster', and perhaps this comes closer to the Mandingo description of a 'jali' than the term blues man does.

At the same time, though, I had found so much that was different. When I listened to Jali Nyama's performances again, and to the songs of a halam player I'd recorded named Abdoulie Samba, I was surprised to hear how much Arabic influence there was in the music. The elaborate instrumental flourishes were all more Arabic than African. Some of the things I heard in it were also common to another Arabic influenced style, the flamenco music of Spain. The kind of intensely brilliant instrumental passages that Jali Nyama played were like the guitar solos in a flamenco performance, and in Samba's playing there was display of virtuosity using nearly every kind of technique that the flamenco players used. When the blues first came to the notice of European intellectuals in the 1920s and 1930s there had been some comment about similarities between the blues and flamenco music but I hadn't taken them seriously because I couldn't see any kind of link between the two styles. It was clear now that the West African musicians had already been influenced by Arabic music just as gypsy singers and instrumentalists had been along the Mediterranean. The influence hadn't come from the Gypsies to the Mississippi blues men. There had been earlier Arabic music that had influenced them both. This would also help explain the Portuguese fado – which is often described as a kind of blues. The songs I heard suggested that both the music of today's griots and the bluesmen had the same common ancestry. What happened to them is that the griots' songs had gone through a long period of exposure to music from the desert and the north. During this same period the music that the slaves had brought to the United States went through a similar exposure to the music of new cultures. Because of the forced isolation of Afro-American culture the music they created still had many African elements, but there was much of it that reflected the new environment.

I often asked Jali Nyama about the old way of singing, and he said to me one day that there was a singer in the village from Mali who sang much older songs. We walked through the village and found the compound where the man was staying. He was a Serrehule, and he played a larger version of the halam called the konting. He was obviously a master musician and within a few minutes the courtyard of the compound was filled with listeners, including a young woman who stood in the shadows holding a glistening fish that she was supposed to be cooking for her husband's lunch. His name was Alhaji Amara Sahone, and like most Serrehules he had traveled considerably. He had been as far as Paris with a traditional instrumental group, and he had an amplifier and an electric pickup for his konting if he needed to play for large audiences. His music, however, hadn't picked up anything on its travels. It was much less ornamented than the music of the coastal griots – it was direct and insistent. He played with a rolling accompaniment style that reminded me a great deal of the old mountain styles of banjo playing in Virginia or Kentucky.

The first piece that he sang was a narrative called 'Bowdi', and here I felt I had come the closest to the feeling and the musical coloring of the blues. He narrated, rather than sang, but in the understatement of the talking voice there was some of the halting persuasiveness of the oldest blues. The accompaniment pattern was shaped around the beating of his thumb on the skin head of the konting, and it extended for two 4/4 measures. The syncopation of the rhythm he plucked on the strings gave it a kind of impetus that I hadn't felt in the more florid griot styles along the coast. It was an austere music. It came from the interior, hundreds of miles from the ocean. It was from this area that most of the slaves had come and in 'Bowdi' I could hear some of the elements of the music that they had brought with them.

12

A Sense Of Something Older

As I looked at the tapes and notes that lay over the dirty concrete floor of the room I understood, finally, that in the blues I hadn't found a music that was part of the old African life and culture. Things in the blues had come from the tribal musicians of the old kingdoms, but as a style the blues represented something else. It was essentially a new kind of song that had begun with the new life in the American South. I still was interested in the music of Mali. The songs that Alhaji Amara Sahone had performed seemed to suggest that there was a different musical style there along the Niger River. When I came to Mali, however, I found that there had been so much contact with the radio and with the musicians from the coast that the brief glimpse I'd had of Mali's music was misleading. The kora players in Mali used some of the same elaborations as the jali from Senegal and The Gambia, the halam and konting players had the same techniques in their accompaniments. Also the people who were now along the coast had been the people who had lived in the interior when the Europeans came. It was only after the arrival of the Europeans and the weakening of the Arab empires that the African societies had wheeled around away from the desert to meet the new arrivals in their ships. This had taken place after the slave trade had begun, and the peoples who had been part of this early movement were the villagers I'd already met on the coast.

I found, however, that Mali had something else to give me. It was still part of the past, despite the modernization that had overtaken its new cities. I wanted to get away from the coast. I wanted to get away from the sea port cities the Europeans had built. I wanted to find something that would give me a sense of an older Africa. It was this that I found in Mali.

The journey to Mali from Banjul began – like everything else – in Banjul's market place. There was the same press of people, the same light sound of women's voices, the same smells of spices and cooking meat and dank concrete. Inside the gate was an old man sitting on a mat against the wall. He usually could locate anything you needed. Could he get me some Senegal francs? The men who usually change money hadn't come yet, but he could find someone for me. He turned and said something to one of the boys who were always loitering around the market. The boy scurried off, and a few moments later a young man in a sport shirt and neatly pressed trousers came through the stalls. One pocket was bulging with folded bundles of tattered, greasy Senegalese francs. After a few moments of serious haggling I had enough currency to get me to Dakar, a day's journey by boat and by road. Mali was so poor that there were no consular offices outside the country, and the only way I could get a visa was to apply in Dakar. From Dakar it was possible to get to Mali by plane, and there was also a railroad line – one of the few in West Africa – that had twice-weekly trains to Bamako, Mali's capital.

From the market place I walked along the river to the ferry landing below my hotel room. To travel to Dakar I had to cross the river, and I'd been told that I could get a truck there that would take me further north. A ferry landed from the other shore and, with a line of other travelers, I bought a ticket at a rusted window grating along a dirty ramp. At the end of the ramp we climbed over the railing onto the ferry boat. It was a low wooden barge with an open deck. A rickety wooden platform of white painted rough boards had been nailed together several feet above the deck so the captian had a kind of bridge to steer from. Behind him on the platform were a few rows of benches and I climbed up there to look down on what was happening on the deck. I stuffed my shoulder bags out of the way under the bench. Most of the people getting on had bundles and suitcases and cardboard cartons and animals so they stayed on the lower deck, but it had no seats, only the railing that circled the deck's open space. The lack of organization became more and more acute as we waited for the ferry to fill with passengers. The confusion was mostly without ill-feeling and there seemed to be a kind of resigned acceptance of it, but the departure was certainly disorganized.

Since the railing was the only place to sit the first people on the deck filled the railing. For the next hour each newcomer had to talk someone along the railing into getting up so that he could climb onto the deck himself. Tempers began to unravel, it grew steadily hotter, the deck slowly filled with heaped-up parcels and cloth wound bundles and rope tied suitcases. When the deck was completely filled the captain of the ferry – an old, very dark-skinned man in a dirty cap and a stifling old tweed overcoat that draped itself limply over his shoulders as a badge of office – pulled on battered levers, shouted orders down to the grease-covered boys who were the ferry's crew, and we backed ponderously into the river's current. After a tentative series of stops and starts we ground to a halt again on a concrete ramp leading down from the street. We had traveled about thirty yards.

Angry voices and new turbulence on the deck below. The boys from the crew were forcing everybody to move so that a car could come on. The ferry's battered wooden bow was slowly being lowered to the concrete ramp on the shore. The shouting rose in volume, the car rattled on, and with a ceaseless blaring of its horn began pushing its way through the dense crowd. Women protested shrilly as they pulled bundles and boxes out of the way, younger men slapped at the car's fenders and sides at it pressed against them. The car finally came to a stop in the center of the angry crowd and the driver, an African, but better dressed than any of the other passengers, jumped out and continued the argument he'd begun with the horn. It was almost a cliché for all the difficulties of bringing modern devices into the agreeable jumble of West African village individualism; its saving characteristic, the final resigned acceptance which somehow made all the confusion finally work.

The captain pushed the signal crank down to alert the engineer below, then vigorously worked at the wheel, which was connected to the rudder by chains that had worn deep troughs into the boards in front of me. The ferry shook with the chugging of the motor, gathered speed – and crashed straight backwards into the pier we'd just pulled away from. People began shouting again, some had fallen off the railing into the water and were being helped back onto the boat. The crewmen hurried to see what damage had been done. The captain cranked his signals again and we veered off into the stream. The ferry seemed undamaged – only a wooden beam splintered on the pier. The captain straightened his shoulders under his sagging coat and turned the wheel over to a teenager in shorts who steered us across the wide mouth of the river.

Despite everything we do to rivers along their banks, there is a sense of timelessness to their drifting current. The Gambia must have looked just about the same to the tribesmen crossing it in wooden canoes as it did to us on the ferry boat. The drift of the water was broad, slow, hazy — moving against us like a lapping tongue. As the old ferry pitched and creaked we wavered along the murky line where the brown current of the mud from upstream nudged against the green swirl of the sea. From the middle of the stream the land looked flat and ragged, with a dark line of trees outlined against the sky. Upstream the river had the breadth and still distances of a bay. Everything was flat, limitless, without dimension or end, only the shining surface of the water and the receding line of palms and brush on the strip of beach behind us.

The village of Bara on the other bank was a straggling line of bleached one-storey stucco buildings. The British had also built a fort on the point closest to the sea, but its white painted walls were crumbling and empty. A rotting wooden pier projected out into the river, with a sloping wooden ramp running down into the water. The captain of the ferry pushed back the flopping sleeves of his overcoat and took over the steering again. With much rattling of cranks and chains and shouts to the crewmen he succeeded in grounding the ferry on the pier. He lowered the bow so we could get off, but there was still a foot and a half of water to be waded through. I clutched my bags and climbed the wooden timbers of the pier. They were already thick with men from the village who were snatching at our luggage. The most determined had leaped down onto the deck and were bargaining with the passengers over the price for carrying their bundles.

A cleared parking area in front of the small collection of houses was filled with vehicles of all sizes and states of repair, with beggars, women selling food, and aggressive teenagers fighting for baggage to carry or demanding money. Whatever else the African societies have taken from the industrialized countries, they have taken over the uncertain way of life reserved for teenagers without jobs. They hung at the fringes of the vehicles shouting at everyone who passed. The boys who had jobs selling tickets for one of the cars or trucks thrust the sheaf of tickets in your face, pulling at your clothes. Everything seemed to be swirling past at once and I could hear snatches of every language along the coast – Mandingo, Wollof, Fula, English, French. A man from one of the trucks began talking to me in rapid, accented French. 'Dakar?' I asked. The vehicles from here go only to a town called Koalak, half way to Dakar. I have to get another truck from there. 200 Senegal francs – about ninety cents – another 100 francs to put my bags on the roof of the truck. Even though I'm inside the cab of the truck the teenagers still hang close to me, plucking at me. 'Why you no give me money?' a boy in a ragged shirt demands. 'Joe, that man goin' steal you,' pointing to the driver, 'You watch. Now you give me shilling for that.' My sleeve is twisted, faces lean in the window. The driver moves the truck to the oil stained concrete of a small gasoline station and they run after me, and gather around the window again. I can see other boys pestering travelers in the other trucks – anyone who isn't in ragged clothes. I'm the only white person in the crowd, but I'm not pursued more assiduously than anyone else. What will these boys be like when they're ten years older? I can already feel a genuine hostility in their demands. Without something else to do beside hang around this knot of vehicles they'll become angrier, harder, and it will be even more difficult to bring them into their own society. They were still shouting at me as the driver finally pulled away on the twisting road north to Senegal.

A long journey functions on many levels of reality and response – but there is so much to it that's simply mechanical that on one level it has some of the characteristics of a large, unwieldy machine that has to be continually tinkered with. I spent the short time I had in Dakar tinkering with the visas and tickets I needed to get to Mali. Dakar, despite its beauty and its comforts, made me feel a little uncomfortable. After the trips back into the countryside the wide sidewalks and the outdoor cafes of Dakar seemed too European – still alien to the land and the people – even though most of the faces were African, even in the restaurants where I went in the morning for croissants and tea. Despite the lack of repairs on the main buildings and the over-crowding in the poor areas, Dakar is a beautiful city, but its culture seems to have so little relationship to the people themselves. In the richer neighborhoods I stood with the beggars and looked over the gates into the beach clubs where the Europeans swam. Around the pools the bodies sunbathing were white; the faces of the men serving them were black. The beggars and I stood obsequiously aside as the gates opened and elegant sports cars were driven out into the streets. Later, as I walked, I saw the sports cars I'd noticed at the pool parked beside the mansions in Dakar's European area. The city, even with its good French cooking and its bookstores and its markets, continued to depress me, and I stayed only long enough to get the forms for the visa approved at the small upstairs office Mali maintained on one of the boulevards near the Presidential Palace.

I'd just missed the train to Bamako, and rather than wait three days for the next one I decided to travel there by plane, see the countryside and the Niger River from the air, and then take the train down. The papers I needed were stamped, I had a last eclair from a patisserie close to the main square, and found a taxi that would take me out to the airport.

Dakar is on the sea – another of the ports the Europeans built to land their ships – and a haze had blown inland from the water. The ground below the plane was only a mottled brown presence glimpsed fitfully through the haze. Then the cloud cover began to thin and by the time we'd reached the barren, pocked ledges of the plateau marking the edge of the Niger basin the land was clear beneath us. The fist-shaped clumps of stone began to give way to dark specks of trees; then to a thin wash of green marking the first patches of grass. The green darkened into a sweep of plain along the gnarled fingers of the Niger, still a threaded maze of tributaries winding themselves into the thickening strand of the river itself. As the plane came lower I could see huts and fields scattered along the river's edge. On the other side of the river from Bamako – where the plane landed several miles to the south – the grass stretched in high, wavering stands between the dark leaved trees. The huts were mostly Mandingo, made of mud, the roofs thatched with dried grass. The small fields beside the buildings had been hacked out of the earth by hand and were still covered with yellowing grain crops.

But it was the Niger I was waiting to see – at last the Niger. As I came close to it in an old taxi I could see that it was brown and muddied, as I'd expected, but when we reached the banks I saw that there was an opaque, greenish gleam to the water. It was as broad as I'd expected, but it was swiftly flowing. The current rushed past dragging clumps of grass and weeds and floating tree trunks with it, even though the valley around me was flat. I had thought, from the river's broad, arching sweep on maps, that it would be sluggish its whole length. I could see, looking back toward Senegal that a line of hills marked its course, and it was the streaming of its tributaries down off the higher level of the hills that gave the river its swiftness. The channel itself was marked with small grassy islands that wove the water around them into surging, ribbed streams. A long, low bridge crossed the Niger and led us into the city.

At first Bamako seemed to be europeanized. It had been built by the French, and it had some of the characteristics of French colonialism I'd seen in Senegal, but it had a different atmosphere. There were more trees, the streets were wide and dusty. Close to the river there were blocks of houses shadowed under a dark canopy of trees. The buildings on most of the streets were single storey and there were gardens and low hanging branches on the side streets. There were people everywhere, walking, riding bicycles, but there was still room to walk on the sidewalks. In the streets were the usual flocks of taxis hurrying after each other like pigeons who had caught sight of someone throwing out food. Men in flowing traditional robes and plastic crash helmets buzzed past on motor scooters.

The main streets of the small city were crowded with traffic, even though the sidestreets were half empty. It was nearly noon and people were on their way home to eat lunch. The taxi pushed its way through the traffic maze and finally brought me to a run down stucco building with a hotel sign on it. The driver thought I could get a room there. The hotel did have an empty room: a boy in ragged clothes showed me to a bare plaster chamber with light blue painted walls that had become fingered and streaked as far up as arms could reach. In the shadows I could dimly make out the ribbed vault of the ceiling twenty feet above me. The bed sagged nearly to the floor as I lay down on it and just over my head was a grimy electric fan. Its three blades were bent up at the ends as if it had been part of an airplane that had crashed through the roof. I put my bags beside the bed and tried to sleep until the worst of the heat had passed.

I found, after only a day walking Bamako's streets, that despite my first impressions, it was different from the cities I'd seen along the coast. It was often only a question of degree since the cultures were similar. It wasn't that Bamako was small. With 200,000 inhabitants it was much larger than Banjul, even if the population was scattered along the riverbank. Unlike the coastal cities, however, it hadn't been put on a sand bank or at a river mouth where ships could land. It was part of the countryside, it could grow more naturally, and at its edges were small farms and the beginnings of villages. I could also feel its isolation − I didn't have the consciousness that it was dominated by outside forces as much as other cities. The pressures on them to become part of a larger economic system seemed to be weaker here. It was harder to come to Bamako, and for the major economic interests there wasn't much to come for; so it had been spared some of what was happening to Lagos or Accra or Freetown.

At the same time Bamako was noisily alive, with a jumbled market area that seemed to be entirely its own creation. Down the narrow alleyways I could see stands and stalls of every kind. In one dirt passageway there were racks of bicycle tires − in another bicycle frames and spare parts. On wide, cracked sidewalks were rows of wildly decorated cheap metal bed frames. The metal panels at the head and feet were painted with iridescent greens or blues and ornamented with colored stripes or tackily done palm trees. On the corners men in from the desert sat with piles of weaving, beside them women crouched patiently with cardboard cartons of drinking glasses. The carnival went on for block after block. Children, nervous goats, and the herd of buzzing motor scooters with their serious robed and helmeted riders plunged past me as I stood back against the buildings and watched. The simplicity of the goods put on display, their obvious utilitarian quality, made it seem more like necessities were being exchanged instead of manufactured goods being sold. It was this also that gave the city its feeling of difference.

I walked, first to the river, despite the lingering heat. I went slowly through littered streets past the rain streaked stucco of old colonial buildings under the folded grasp of large trees. People in wrinkled, dirt stained robes were sleeping in shelters under the bushes in small parks, their charcoal fires still smoking from their meager breakfasts. Along the banks of the river the sun's heat seemed to gather itself as it was reflected up from the water's glistening, gray-green surface, but despite the heat dozens of men were washing clothes. Their arms thrust the clothes into the water; then swung them up in a streaming circle to pound them down against the rocks that protruded from the water's edge. Since they had no soap they were beating the dirt out of the clothes. On the patch of grass above the bank there were hundreds of shirts and pairs of pants spread out to dry. They were Bamako's laundrymen.

One thing that had struck many of the travelers throughout the Bambara area was the muscular symmetry of the men's bodies. I had read over and over again something like, 'As the oarsmen drove their canoes through the surging current one could not help admiring the strength of biceps and shoulders, which gave the dark bodies a kind of rude poetry as they leaned into their task ...'

Despite the incongruity of the work they were doing the men's bodies had this kind of wiry strength. Most of them were tall and wide-shouldered, their upper bodies tapering to thin waists. Their skin was very dark, almost black in tone. The exercise they got swinging wet shirts against the stones gave them the same supple masculinity they had had a hundred years ago as warriors. Beyond them I could see the same lean, wide-shouldered bodies of boatmen as they stood in their log canoes pulling at brushwood tangled in the grass of a small island close to the bank. Except for all that laundry spread out on the grass the scene had the exaggerated romance of a 19th century engraving from a travel book.

As I walked away from the river Bamako itself seemed to have some of this quality of an engraving from an old book. It was still a trading place, still a meeting place. Men hurried by with bundles, women wrapped in colorful skirts stared at me curiously when I came toward the stalls. The few other foreigners sitting in cafes or walking along under the trees were hardly noticed. From time to time I saw musicians, and in this isolated, still backward city they walked along with their robes swinging, hardly looking at anyone around them. A boy, lagging a few steps behind, carried their koras. One passed me riding on a bicycle with his kora slung down his back.

The market place in the center of the town had this same feeling of being from another time, despite the racks of shirts from Hong Kong and the plastic shopping bags that festooned the stalls lining its outside walls. Inside it the light was dim and the air cool. The stone floor was heaped with woven lengths of cloth or blue and white patterned desert rugs and crudely made sandles. In one row of arches there were old men selling gold dust, in another lines of weathered statues and carelessly heaped up silver necklaces. I realized that I could find anything I wanted in the market, if I just looked patiently enough. The bargaining went on without rancour or haste, and I soon learned that although nearly everyone spoke some French they didn't speak much more than I did and it was possible to converse enough to make any kind of purchase.

What I finally emerged with, however, did typify some of the confusions and contradictions I had found everywhere on my journey. For the better part of two days I bargained and haggled over handwoven materials that filled one section of the market. I finally chose lengths of grayish ribbed cotton cloth that had been sewn together from sections made on small village looms. I bought skirt materials that combined strips of strong, simple cotton weaving with thin strips of elaborate band weaving in contrasting colors. After an afternoon of selection and discussion with a small, patient man who had a large pile of rugs I found a traditional pattern in blue and white wool and we reached an eventual agreement on the price. Then when I came to leave the market with my pile of exultantly colorful hand woven materials the only thing I could find to carry them in was one of the striped plastic shopping bags hanging from the stalls outside.

I found some of the same incongruities when I talked with the musicians. When I went out into Bamako's streets after dark I could hear music in dance places and over the radio, but it was modern music that dominated almost everywhere. Because of the popularity of the musicians, they were part of Bamako's everyday life, and the kora playing had the same flourishes I'd heard in Banjul and Dakar. They were master musicians who had made their singing and playing part of their own modern world.

13

The Bamako-Dakar
International Express

The Niger curves to the north and east as it streams through Bamako – shaping itself into the great sweeping curve that leaves its strong mark on the maps of West Africa. The direction of its current – eastward into the interior – had confused Europeans, and it was this that Mungo Park had been most anxious to learn as he approached its banks. Even after Park had determined that the river existed and that it flowed eastward, however, it was difficult for cartographers to decide what it did next. The usual decision was to trace its passage eastward to the Nile. The Niger curves to the south again and empties into the Atlantic in eastern Nigeria, but its mouth is such a maze of small silt-filled channels that the early travelers had missed it completely. On Park's second journey he was trying to follow the river's course by boat and he had begun the turn to the south when he was killed by tribesmen after a squabble over tribute.

A day's truck journey to the east of Bamako was the town of Segou, which had been the name of the town where Park had first seen the Niger, and was one of the river's old settlements. I was interested enough in Park to want to see it, but even more I wanted to see some place that was older. Everything I had seen in West Africa, even Bamako, had been built in recent times. The villages I had seen in the countryside had been moved and shifted, huts had been torn down and replaced. At Segou I was told I could see a part of the town that had been there before the French came. I rode out to the depot for the little passenger trucks on the other side of the river, sat in the sun waiting for one to fill up; then we set out on the paved road that crossed the open, sweeping land south of the river. Most of the countryside was dry and empty, but at the end of the afternoon, with the shadows of the palms stretching casually across the roadway as we passed, we came to the river again and to the first village on Segou's outskirts.

Around me was a different atmosphere. The buildings in the villages were made of solid mud that had been baked by the sun, and they were surrounded with tilled fields that seemed to have been there for centuries. Along the dirt paths women and children were hurrying from building to building with jars balanced on their heads. It was – as I recognized – an Africa that had been influenced by Arab cultures. The way of life it represented was as much of an imposition as the European cities were along the coast – it was only a different kind of imperialism – but it still gave me what I had wanted to experience, a sense of continuity with the past. It was this that I had experienced with the griots, a consciousness of a continuing culture. The same sense was here around me, in the rounded walls of the houses, in the earthen ditches beside the fields, in the swaying crests of the palms, whose years hung heavily over them.

Trying again to put myself in the place of someone from another tribe – as I'd done in Amara Sahe's compound – with a set of cultural conditionings that were simply different from those of the tribes around me, not more advanced or less advanced, I realized that my response to the atmosphere of age in these dusty villages reflected a European and American concern with the old – buildings, towns, cathedrals, farmhouses. A facile generalization could be made that as we have become more and more uneasy about the continuity of our cultures and societies we lean more heavily on those physical objects which clearly reflect the historical past we find more and more difficult to believe in. Whatever the reasons, the absence of physical survivals from the past has always been disappointing to travelers in West Africa. What they didn't grasp was that the continuity came within the culture itself – in language, ceremony, and belief. Since they almost never learned enough of the languages around them to understand this longer cultural movement they decided it wasn't there – not realizing that any society has to have this paraphenalia to enable it to project itself into the future – and by this continue its way of life and justify its own place in the future.

So I could say that my response to these sun-baked, mud-toned buildings was a conditioning of my own cultural background – but at the same time it seemed also to say that something could be preserved, even if so much else that I had met in West Africa seemed to be threatened by even more hurried changes and an uncertain future. The songs I had found weren't enough of a barricade, and language itself had proved too fragile to bear the weight of reinforcing a cultural consciousness – the river and the fields and the villages were a support for a more solid structure.

Segou itself was a blending of French colonial buildings erected in the 1920's or '30's, and heavy streets of earthen buildings, their facades flowing together into a kind of elongated hive. The dark doorways opened into shadowy interiors that seemed to contain an infinite distance within them, even though the river's green shining form flashed by a short distance behind the houses. On two or three of the dirt streets weavers had stretched their colorful warp of thread in front of them as they sat under sun shelters woven from leaves and operated the spindles with their fingers and the toes of their bare feet. Since the culture had never developed a frame to take up the remaining warp it was stretched twenty or thirty yards in front of the weaver, held tight with stone weights. As he worked he dragged it toward him through the dust. In small shelters along the sides of the streets I could see other craftsmen – sandle makers and metal workers. I could feel some of the continuities I'd experienced in Bamako – that this river town, in its isolation, still had a vitality of its own. It was difficult to say how long it could be maintained, since the fragile structures of these communities give way so quickly to newer technologies, but it was present now. As I walked through the narrow streets in the oldest parts of the town, staying close to the earth walls to take advantage of whatever shade they offered, I realized that the experience of these Niger towns like Segou gave me a measure with which I could gauge some of the other things I had seen in Africa.

Just as I was later to measure much of what I experienced in West Africa against my feelings in Segou the journey back to the coast by train – nearly 1000 miles on the 'Bamako-Dakar International Express' – was to be the standard against which I measured all the traveling I'd done. It was immediately obvious when I straggled through the dirt following the stream of other passengers to the station at seven in the morning that the term 'International Express' was a little misleading. A line of dirty, old-fashioned railway cars stood at the station platform with a flood of people washing against it. The last cars in the line were rusted, windowless freight carriages to transport a herd of goats who were huddled together at the end of frayed ropes staring anxiously at the crowds hurrying past them. People were eddying in and out of the dark portals of the station and in the sidling currents the ubiquitous vendors drifted past with baskets of bread, fruit, roots, and fans wavering on turning heads.

There was a sleeping car at the end of the train, but I had decided to ride in the coaches. I had some bread and canned fruit I'd bought in the market, and I'd brought a bottle of water with me from the hotel. The coach, with windows open and doors dangling onto the station platform, was painted dark green with a low white ceiling. Over the aisle hung eight white painted fans like a line of small round clouds. The noise of the passengers struggling to get their things settled filled the narrow space, but the mood was patient and cheerful. The dark faces around me were smiling. We exchanged greetings in uncertain French. Robes were hitched under arm pits as arms lifted, lifted, lifted and the car visibly settled under the weight of suitcases, bundles, boxes, and piles of sticks jammed into luggage racks. The bundles were wrapped in the same colored cloth as the robes and the turbans of the people lifting them, and the lengths of dyed fabric stood out against the mottled green of the car sides and dirty red torn plastic of the seats with their startling splashes of orange, blue, and yellow.

For a time the confusion over seat numbers threatened to overwhelm us. We each had a seat reservation – it was required at the time the ticket itself was purchased – but only a handful of people around me could read. The numbers didn't mean anything. The arguments were more resigned or exasperated than angry. There seemed to be a recognition that some sort of system was intended, even if it was incomprehensible. Bundles were shifted, suitcases were lifted down from the racks, bundles of sticks were pushed along the aisle. The sticks were an aromatic wood used for teeth cleaning, and the people bringing them would sell them when the train got to Dakar. My own seat had already been taken over by a harrassed young family so I found a place to sit on the aisle in the midst of a group of Mandingo women who were talking excitedly among themselves. The pans of food and water that each woman had brought had already been passed back and forth, and women with babies squirmed through the now jammed aisles looking for any seat that was still empty. The conductors patiently looked at tickets, climbed over bundles to look at seat numbers, pushed packages more firmly into baggage racks. Swarming flies lazily searched through the bundles along the ceiling and already the roaches were picking through the debris at our feet.

Somehow watermelons had come in through the windows and had been carefully placed on top of all the other things that had been packed into the coach. Everywhere I looked on the floor and under the seats I could see ripe watermelons. Like the bundles of sticks they were for the markets in Dakar. The confused jostling went on without rancor, the dominant sound a continual laughter, like a sentence without an ending. I was the only foreigner in the coach, but the other passengers were used to the occasional French student who traveled alone as I was doing and I was included in any offer of food as plates and dishes went from hand to hand. A sudden jerking spilled some of the food, there was a metallic clanging, and the International Express crawled hesitantly away from the din of the station two hours late.

I was still under the impression that I was on an ordinary – if somewhat disorganized – train journey, and I stretched back in my seat, watching the landscape crawl by out of the open window. Seventeen minutes after we left the station – I'd noticed the time on my wristwatch – the International Express stopped again at the top of the long rise leading away from the Niger. Outside the window there was a sudden bobbing of yellow – a frenzied yellow – green blooming. Hundreds of women were running toward the train with baskets of guavas on their heads. I was used to people selling things to passengers on passing trains, but the women around me were suddenly standing up, leaning out the windows, waving to the women outside. I looked on, puzzled, as a frenzied bidding and bargaining went on. A woman leaning over my shoulder to get to the window gestured impetuously and a woman with a basket of guavas gave her one to taste. I still didn't understand until the woman tasting the guava bargained more intently, nodded her head, and then reached out a basket. The woman outside the train emptied all the fruit she was carrying into the basket and handed it back. At this point all semblance to a train journey ended. Guavas rained in through the windows, guavas poured in through the doors.

Around me women had produced bags and boxes and cartons. I found myself standing up holding bags open so that my neighbors could pour guavas into them. The car filled with the sweet stench of the small round fruit.

Money came from its hiding places all around me. The woman sitting with me – in flowing blue lace robe over flowered underblouse, a heavy, imposing woman of considerable dignity, one wrist ringed with gold bracelets – fumbled in her brassiere as she leaned out to shout. Her money was in tattered bills tied in a dirty handkerchief to her brassiere strap. Guavas streamed in through the windows and there was still a waving golden field of guavas in baskets borne on the heads of the women outside. Guavas piled up on the platforms of the car, guavas covered over the watermelons. Guavas were everywhere. Boxes and bags of them filled the aisles and the space between the seats. Finally the woman beside me settled back counting coins and measuring the contents of her cloth sacks. She nodded, satisfied, held up fingers and said, 'Mil cinq cent francs.' 1500 Mali francs. About $3 in American money. There was still a yellow wavering outside the window, but the International Express finally gathered itself and lurched away, exuding a perfume of ripe, sweet guava.

Around me guavas were being sampled, dumped, heaped, pushed under seats as the women talked noisily and excitedly. For them the Bamako-Dakar International Express was a kind of traveling market. Just as traders had traveled through the countryside years before with their goods heaped on the backs of camels and donkeys the women rode the train, heaped up goods as they went along and counted their money until they had a chance to sell some of what they were buying. I talked with the woman next to me who, now that she had started buying, had become more relaxed and expansive. She would take the fruit she was buying into Senegal and sell it there. What would she do to get home, I asked her. She laughed. She would use her money to buy canned goods in Dakar, and she would sell them out the train windows on her way back. She rode the train back and forth – nearly a thousand miles each way – buying and selling as she went. It was part of a trade network that had sprung up along the railroad. I wasn't taking a train ride – I was journeying with a caravan.

Thirty minutes after we left the crest of the hill, the International Express slowed down and came to a stop in another sea of fluttering baskets. Guavas poured in through the windows – and now there were squash, melons, onions – a half bushel of white peppers was shoved under my seat. I held bags open, I handed baskets back and forth, I helped lift cartons into the aisle. I was simply accepted as part of the jumble. The lady next to me was on her feet again untying her bundle of money. She counted out bills, she counted boxes and bags – sitting again she used her fingers to check her figures and nodded, satisfied. 'Trois cent francs.' Three hundred francs, about 60 cents. The International Express grated forward again in its cloud of perfume from the guavas, and the sorting, shifting, tasting went on again. We slid down a long slope of brush and trees as the air streaming in through the windows mingled its smells of earth and drying grass with the smells of guavas, of onions, and of aromatic sticks.

The stops went on. As we came into wooded country we began to take on more bundles of sticks and yams. The platforms of the car were stuffed with tobacco leaves, the toilets were filled with cartons of guavas. Later in the afternoon there was a stop where the women who ran up to the train brought only food. The caravan travelers leaned out this time to buy bread dipped in sauce, spiced chicken, bananas, oranges, and cooked yams. My own journey to the coast seemed embarrassingly trivial compared to the gusto and energy everywhere around me. I wondered if I shouldn't try to buy something myself to sell further down the line. By this time I was sitting with my feet on guavas, with boxes of guavas up to my elbows in the aisles, with my own bags propped on a heap of guavas. The International Express lumbered on so slowly it was difficult to believe that it would ever manage to finish its journey.

By the middle of the night almost as many people had crowded into the aisles as there were in the seats and there were long, careful searches in the cars at the border into Senegal. The train personnel went up and down the aisles, clambering over the sticks and the cartons and the bags and the bundles. Their progress was as slow and as painstaking as someone climbing a mountainside. There were arguments now, people confused about their tickets and their seats. The conductors perched on the heaped goods in the aisle and slowly sorted out the problems. I understood again something I had learned about African men along the coast. One of the virtues expected of the man is that he can resolve disputes. The ideal man is one who can keep peace in his compound and can quiet the quarreling of his wives. The conductors had this combination of care and persistent patience, and after a while I realized that the shrillness from the women as they shouted at each other was only partly serious. They clearly expected a man to come along and solve the problem. I had once asked a man in a village if this difference between the man's role in these kinds of disputes had made it more difficult for the colonial commissioners who had to settle some of these quarrels in their districts. 'Oh yes,' the man said and laughed, 'The African man wants to find a way to solve the problems, but the Europeans just tried to tell us what was right and wrong.'

I slept a little as the train journeyed to the coast. About midnight there was another food stop and I ran out into the darkness and bought something from a shadowed, boiling pot – seeing when I got back into the light that what I had on my plate were bits of boiled kidney. In the morning the train stopped outside a small village because of a break in the rail line. With the villagers we all walked ahead to watch a track crew trying to lay new rails. They had only shovels and a sledge hammer for driving spikes, but after all the excitements of the day before it seemed only to be expected that a handful of workers with a few battered tools could get a heavy locomotive and a line of railroad cars over a break in the rails. The rail lengths had expanded in the heat so the workers had to shift the roadbed to adjust to the new curve. They shoveled stones from one side of the rails to the other, working steadily despite the heat, and after an hour they waved to the engineer to come ahead. Again with the same natural acceptance of the difficulties of a train journey we all walked alongside as the train slowly rode on the new roadbed over the modest heaps of shoveled gravel. It stopped a hundred yards beyond and waited for us to climb back into the cars so it could lurch off on its journey again.

The day drifted past. As soon as the train was on its way, the traders around me had become busy again. But this time they were selling. I stood up and poured guavas out of bags into empty baskets that women had brought outside the train. The level of guavas that had flooded the car slowly receded. The woman beside me tied and untied her pouch of money as she zealously sold guavas and onions at every stop. The caravan, its load lightened, seemed to go faster, and we began to see the roads and the stucco buildings of central Senegal. I was leaving the train at the town of Koalak so that I could go down again into The Gambia, and as I stood up with my bags the women around me smiled and waved and called out *Bon jour* in light, still laughing voices. I stood in the shadows of the station and watched the bargaining and selling going on the length of the train. When the train slowly pulled away I half expected to see a line of camels plodding stolidly on at the end of it. The caravan driver on the last platform lazily waved to me with his signal lantern and the clanking caravan slid out of sight.

14

A Bridge Over The Niger

With the rattle of the small connecting train taking me to Koalak my trip was over. I had opened each one of the nest of boxes I had brought with me in my luggage. I had opened each of them one by one and looked at what was inside it. I had received a thousand impressions; some things had become clearer, others in their way had become more obscure and difficult to grasp. I had read as I'd traveled, I'd talked with people everywhere I'd gone, I'd heard so many things about Africa that it threatened to dissolve in front of my eyes. It was as if I'd built up something out of wet sand, and as it dried the individual grains casually detached themselves from the heap I'd laboriously piled up and slid down onto the beach.

I found, finally, that there was a last elusive fragment inside the boxes I'd carried with me, one that was the most difficult of all to understand. I have to go back a little in time – only a few days, but back to Bamako. One night I decided to walk across the Niger River bridge just after sunset, when most of the people who lived on the other side of the river from the city were streaming home from work. As I walked toward the river it was still dusk and I could see the shapes of the trucks and cars looming through the dust beside me as I walked. Before I had gone far I had become part of a tide of people, all of us trudging through the darkness, feeling the clouds of dust blow against our clothes and skin, all of us making our way toward the black shape of the bridge. Beside us, in the dimness of the evening, was a line of cars plodding bumper to bumper, the gray haze of exhaust fumes mingling with the dust blowing over the river. It was like some kind of exodus, without panic, but with a grim intensity to it as we hurried on silently.

The traffic slowed at the banks of the Niger since there was only one lane of traffic each way on the long bridge and the stream of cars had to give way to other cars coming from the deeper darkness of side streets. The sidewalk of the bridge was in disrepair, pitted with large holes so that it was dangerous to hurry as we crossed it in the darkness. I made my way slowly until I was standing on the roadway over the bank of the river itself, and I could make out the dimly outlined shapes of the small boats that made their way up and down the river with passengers and freight. There, was a small fire on the deck of one of them and I could see people sitting around it cooking. The river was almost completely shadowed and I could only make out the gray sheen of the water, streaked with yellowing reflections from the passing lights. Downstream, on one of the sloping banks below Bamako, I could see the lights of other small fires that fitfully cast their flickering points of light against the enveloping darkness.

I stood for a long time against the railing letting people stream by. Only a few glanced toward me. There was so much dust mingled with the graying haze of the exhaust fumes that most people were hurrying as quickly as they could to get across the bridge. If they did look at me there was no sign of surprise that I was white. It was no more, or less, unusual for someone like me to be standing there than it would be for someone from Mali to be leaning against the railing of a bridge across the Seine, watching the people of Paris stream home to their apartments. As difficult as the broken pavement was, and as nervous as I was trying to follow the hurrying figures in front of me in the darkness I still wanted to cross the river and I began walking again. There was so much noise from the cars and the feet and the automobile horns that it was impossible to hear the sound of my own feet, and the scene became almost dream-like. I seemed to be moving somewhere outside the experience. I was outside the reality of Africa at the same time as I was immersed in the presence of Africa.

I was conscious that Africa had so many faces, and that each of them was intensely different. I could see the contrasts that are often used to describe West Africa today. I was standing on a modern bridge flooded with cars and hurrying people coming home from their offices, and there below me on the decks of the small river boats were people who were still living in tribal villages, bound to the land in a traditional system of subsistence farming. One of the groups – the people on the bridge – had entered the Twentieth Century and the other still hesitated distrustfully somewhere just beyond the gate. I had read so often about these contrasts that they had become a cliché, like the photographs taken over and over again of camels standing in front of jet airplanes. I was also aware of the other easily perceivable cliché, the sudden collapse of time differences. Only two hundred years after a frightened and half-starving Mungo Park barely managed to drag himself to the Niger's banks, I could get there by taking an airplane. There had been so many changes. Simply by being there – at that place on the bridge at that moment of the evening as the cars clanked past – I was helping to bring about changes myself. There would be more people like me and they would change some place like Mali more than it would change them.

I had all of these clichés in my mind as I stood on the ground on the other side of the bridge and looked down into the water. But it wasn't these things I was conscious of. What suddenly came over me was the realization that all the things I had read and studied about Africa before I'd come, the newspaper articles, the photo texts, the political analyses, the books, the notes – they all had so little to do with Africa. The word appeared again and again, certain places, certain customs were described, photographic symbols appeared again and again to try to lend the texts some credence, but it still had almost nothing to do with Africa. What it had to do with was the society of the person who was writing. Africa was a cliché, a metaphor, a symbol – it was everything but itself.

The central concept in everything that I had read was the obvious one that there had been prolonged contact between the European and African societies, and that African society had been altered as a consequence. The differences came in how the Western writers described these contacts, and the moral decisions they made about the results. To criticize the role of the Europeans in Africa is to criticize European society itself – and everything that is written about Africa becomes part of the bitter debate over what has happened, and what should happen, within the societies of the western world. I had understood from the beginning that this was part of the modern reality, but what I hadn't understood was that the opinions had already been formed, and Africa was simply used as a kind of marker in the unending debates that go on in the European and American political worlds.

In all of this posturing there is little interest in Africa itself. As any educated African has noticed, the only time news from Africa appears in the newspapers of the world is when there are Europeans or

Americans involved, or when there is some development that affects western interests. The changes that are sweeping over Africa, the new society that is emerging in Africa goes unnoticed. Instead there are the clichés and the vague generalities that involve the writers' own societies. It was difficult for me – now that I had come so close to a part of Africa – to make any kind of generalizations. I had learned only that the patterns of change were so complex that it was almost impossible to predict what the Africa of the future would be like, except that it would reflect the bewildering diversity and the strong vitality of the present.

The traffic pushed past me into the darkness, the cars on their way to the new houses that had been built on the river's south bank. I walked on beyond the end of the bridge and watched the traffic stream past. Along the edge of the river I could see the darker shapes of people who would sleep on the earth for the night. They were huddled close to small fires, a few faces turned to look at the cars as they passed. The two kinds of people, in the cars and on the bank, were in a jumbled moment of time, and only the coming years would help them find their own places in it. I had wondered why there was such a strong attraction between the two cultures – the African and the European. There were economic causes – but often the European commercial activities had been unprofitable and uneconomic. There were cultural causes – but in their interrelationships the Africans and the Europeans both lost a part of their cultural identity. But I now understood that there was something else that continued and extended the contacts even when they had become meaningless from any economic sense. The two cultures have an obsessive attraction for each other. For the Americans and the Europeans who have romanticized Africa it represents something that they have lost. A simplicity, a closeness, an emotional directness – all the clichés that people use when they are describing 'Africa'. But the Africans are just as drawn to the West – since it represents something they haven't yet achieved. A technical complexity, a diminishing work burden, and a loosening of the restrictions of clan traditions and family customs – all the clichés that Africans use when they are describing the 'West'.

In the beginning I had been misled by the free use of terms to describe the interaction between the two cultures – terms that were either bitterly negative or misleadingly positive. All the words used so often – 'exploitation', 'cooperation', 'technical advancement', 'cultural imperialism' – were struggling to describe what was happening as two cultures so different from each other met and interacted. What I should have remembered was that by the simple act of giving something to a subsistence farming group that they can't produce themselves – something as simple as a knife – the whole balance of the society is tipped. What happens next seems to happen as inevitably as the laws of physics – even if the processes could possibly be reversed at some distant moment in time. At this point of modern technological development it would seem that the African tribal, self-sufficient village culture – such as it still exists – is an economic anachronism. But in the next century it could be just as true that the overweighted Western economies, without a close relationship to the land and its resources and without clearly defined social goals could become just as much an anachronism. What I could see was only that a process of change had begun and that it would continue without ceasing and its final results were as difficult to forsee as anything else about Africa and its people.

I had come to Africa to find a kind of song, to find a kind of music and the people who performed it. But nothing can be taken from a culture without considering its context. I had become as involved in this context as I was in the music itself, and I had known from the beginning that it would be the people themselves who would tell me the most about what I'd come to find. I'd come looking for a kind of song, and even if I hadn't really found it, I'd found the people who sang it. The journey I'd begun had taken me to places I hadn't expected, and the ideas and attitudes I had at the end of it were different from where I'd started. But the essence of a journey is its movement from one place to another. For me the journey had become as much a movement from one idea to another as it was a movement through a landscape and its peoples. It was these things I had to carry along with me, along with the tapes and notes in my bags.

As I stood in the darkness on the bridge over the Niger the stream of cars dwindled, the few people still passing me were now wearing sweaters and jackets. The fires along the banks of the river began to dwindle, their small reddish eyes closing as the eyes of the sleepers around them closed. I could see a reflection of distant lights on the dark sheen of the water. It had gotten chilly. The night cold of the desert was creeping along the ground towards Bamako. I buttoned my shirt higher, picked my way through the darkness back over the broken sidewalk of the bridge, and walked slowly and carefully back to the hotel to pack my things so I could leave early the next morning on the International Express from Bamako to Dakar.

Also by Samuel Charters

Poetry
The Children
The Landscape at Bolinas
Heroes of the Prize Ring
Days
To This Place
From a London Notebook
From a Swedish Notebook
In Lagos
Of Those Who Died

Fiction
Mr Jabi and Mr Smythe
Jelly Roll Morton's Last Night at the Jungle Inn
Louisiana Black

Criticism
Some Poems/Poets

Biography, with Ann Charters
I Love (The Story of Vladimir Mayakovsky and Lili Brik)

Translations
Baltics (from the Swedish of Tomas Transtromer)
We Women (from the Swedish of Edith Sodergran)
The Courtyard (from the Swedish of Bo Carpelan)

Music
Jazz: New Orleans
The Country Blues
Jazz: A History of the New York Scene
The Poetry of the Blues
Robert Johnson
The Legacy of the Blues
The Swedish Fiddlers
The Blues Makers